FAIRCHILD REPUBLIC
A-10 THUNDERBOLT II

1972 to date (all marks)

First published in May 2017
Reprinted 2021 (twice), December 2022 and February 2024

A catalogue record for this book is available from the British Library.

ISBN 978 1 78521 081 5

Library of Congress control no. 2016959360

Published by Haynes Group Limited,
Sparkford, Yeovil,
Somerset BA22 7JJ, UK.
Tel: 01963 440635
Int. tel: +44 1963 440635
Website: www.haynes.com

Haynes North America Inc.,
2801 Townsgate Road, Suite 340,
Thousand Oaks, CA 91361, USA.

Printed in India.

Commissioning Editor: Jonathan Falconer
Copy editor: Ian Heath
Proof reader: Penny Housden
Indexer: Peter Nicholson
Page design: James Robertson

Acknowledgements

The author would like to thank the following for their assistance in the creation of this book: Colonel (retired) Philip Haun; Technical Sergeant Sam Confer; and Joachim Jacob.

FAIRCHILD REPUBLIC
A-10 THUNDERBOLT II

1972 to date (all marks)

Owners' Workshop Manual

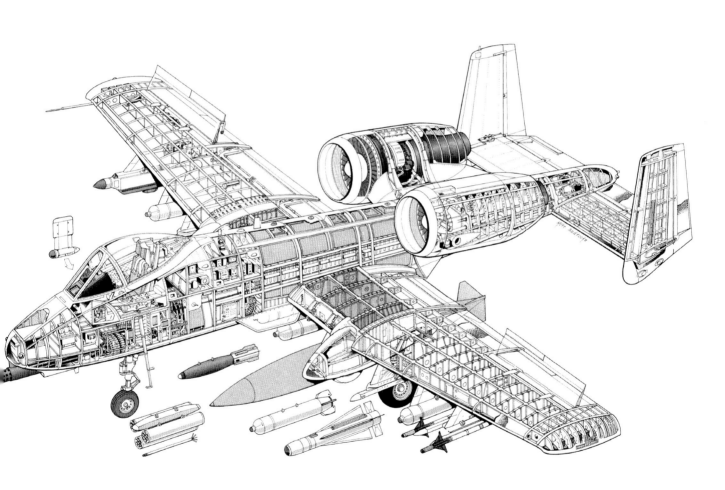

Insights into the design, operation and maintenance of the 'Hog' – the world's undisputed king of close air support

Steve Davies

Contents

BELOW With travel pod loaded, this A-10A from Whiteman Air Force Base, Missouri, returns from a deployment. The FT tail codes identify it as belonging to the 76th Fighter Squadron. *(all photos USAF except where credited otherwise)*

Introduction

Growing up in East Anglia (on the eastern side of the UK) during the Cold War was a mixed blessing. On the one hand, the threat of apocalyptic war always lingered somewhere in your mind and there were little reminders of it everywhere (our rural village even had its own air-raid shelter); but on the other hand the military build-up in the region meant that there was always excitement to be found if you were a young aviation fanatic like me.

Speaking personally, there are two immutable images from those days that are etched into my memory. The first is the SR-71 flying over my village on its way into and out of RAF Mildenhall. The excitement of knowing that it was either returning from or going on a spy mission was almost uncontainable. The second, and I swear this is true, is cycling across the flat Suffolk countryside, miles from any other person, building or machine, and being surprised to see an A-10 flying beneath the electrical wires strung between two distant pylons. That, I thought, is what I want to end up doing.

By January 1979 there was an impressive six-squadron wing operating A-10s out of the twin bases of RAF Bentwaters and RAF Woodbridge on the east coast, so A-10s and their distinctive whine were a common sight. Designed to fly low and kill Soviet main battle tanks, the 'Hog' was a firm favourite of many a school friend. Heck, they even had an A-10 Transformer toy that we all yearned after. That was all a long time ago, and these days there are no A-10s left in Europe, let alone the UK.

Today, I am in the fortunate position of having been able to write about the A-10 professionally. In 2009 and 2016, while reporting for an aviation magazine, I was given unique access to the US Air Force's operational test and evaluation process between the A-10 and F-35. The latter visit occurred at a time when the discussion about which was 'better' was about to hit fever pitch, and when the Air Force really needed to get the F-35 to that important milestone, Initial Operating Capability. I told the operator's story; I let their wisdom and experience speak for itself,

BELOW Gathering snow during an inclement Massachusetts night, an O/A-10A of the 104th FW awaits the next day's sorties. The A-10 has a history of operating in cold climes, and for many years operated out of Eielson AFB, Alaska, where temperatures in winter are extreme.

RIGHT The fans of the twin TF-34s make for excellent radar reflectors – the A-10 was born in an age where a select few were treated to signature reduction techniques and low observable technologies.

avoiding the temptation to interject with my own views too much. It was an approach that most people responded well to, so I've done the same again here.

The questions of whether the A-10 can be or should be replaced, and whether the F-35A is the 'right' airframe to do it with, spark emotional and sometimes illogical responses. With that in mind, I haven't really asked them in this book. The caveat is that I have stated that, historically speaking, there has always been someone trying to cancel or retire the A-10. In fact, I can think of no other modern weapon system that has been so successful yet had so many detractors lobbying for its demise.

Whatever your views are regarding what should happen to the A-10 next, I hope you enjoy this read. As always, you can send feedback to me at www.facebook.com/AviationPhotography/ or contact me on Twitter @AF702389.

Steve Davies, Cambridgeshire, England
December 2016

BELOW Now a resident of the Air Force Museum, Dayton, Ohio, this A-10A wears the markings of the Massachusetts Air National Guard, as deployed to Operation Desert Storm, 1991. The two-tone green 'Lizard' scheme was typical of that worn by NATO aircraft operating in the European theatre during the latter stages of the Cold War.

Chapter One

The Warthog story

There aren't many aircraft that instil such fear into the hearts of the enemy that they gain their own moniker, but the Fairchild Republic A-10 Thunderbolt II is one of the few that does – 'Whispering Death'.

OPPOSITE MD tail codes identify these two A-10As as belonging to the 175th FW, Maryland Air National Guard. Up high, these A-10 pilots will be very carefully managing their energy state, powered as they are by turbofans that gasp for air at such dizzying heights! *(USAF)*

The name 'Whispering Death' was given to the Warthog – or 'Hog', as it is known to those who fly and maintain it – by soldiers of the Iraqi Republican Guard. These elite troops had enforced the will of their dictator, Saddam Hussein, and invaded neighbouring Kuwait in August 1990. The invasion had been a rout despite some courageous resistance from Kuwaiti military units, but when an American-led Coalition arrived in the region and engaged the Iraqi forces in the early hours of 17 January 1991 the victor rapidly became the loser. From on high, A-10s engaged Iraqi armour, infantry and fixed positions, their TF-34 turbofans so quiet that their victims scarcely heard them coming. Whispering Death indeed.

But there was more to this than just a name – the requirements for the A-10 had been written in blood on the battlefields of Vietnam, culminating in 1969 with the US Department of Defense asking defence contractors to submit proposals for a new attack aircraft that could survive the sort of pummelling that the North Vietnamese could dish out day in, day out. Since then the A-10 has lived a tumultuous life – an airframe that

the Air Force had never really wanted. But then, in late 1990, and on the precipice of early retirement, the A-10 finally came alive and silenced its critics, doing at last what it had been born to do. This is its story.

South East Asia – the Vietnam War

Through the 1960s and early 1970s, the United States was engaged in a ground and air war in support of the capitalist government of South Vietnam. Their foe, the communist government of North Vietnam, was fighting a low-tech insurgency war that jarred with American doctrine and technology. America's forces were conventional: built to take on the might of Soviet Russia, not to tackle farmers-turned-warriors in a rice paddy.

From a doctrinal point of view, few things illustrated how ill prepared the US was to fight North Vietnam than its early struggle to provide close air support (CAS). The most numerous fighter in the Air Force's inventory was the Republic F-105 Thunderchief. Big and fast, sure, but not designed to carry lots of ordnance over a fleeting target that often required slow and low flight to find, fix, target and engage. Even the Air Force's newest fighter, the McDonnell F-4C Phantom II, offered little improvement in this regard. Similarly, the Cessna A-37A Dragonfly,

ABOVE, RIGHT AND BELOW The Air Force was a fan of big, fast fighters. The F-4 Phantom II (above), F-105 Thunderchief (centre) and F-100 Super Sabre (below) were all designed to fly high and fast, and to deliver one or more tactical nuclear weapons over a strategic target. In the case of the F-4, it was a dual-role monster that, having originally been designed for the Navy as its Fleet Defender, could also tackle air-to-air missions. None of them was well suited to the CAS role, and the Air Force was not enthusiastic about its air-to-air potential either. *(USAF)*

converted from the T-37A trainer into a lightweight counter-insurgency attack jet, lacked the loiter time necessary to be truly effective in the CAS role.

The situation forced the Air Force to think laterally about the mission and those tasked with executing it. The result was employment of World War Two vintage attack aircraft such as the T-28D and the B-26 in the CAS role.

In all, the Navy's A-1 Skyraider would eventually provide the Air Force with its most solid CAS and CSAR (combat search and rescue capability) asset in the form of the A-1E. The radial-engined aircraft handled well at low speed, carried up to 8,000lb of bombs and could loiter over the forward edge of troops for long durations. But the venerable Skyraider was unquestionably a compromise: it was

ABOVE AND BELOW Getting low to the ground, dodging enemy fire, absorbing enemy fire, being able to fly slowly enough that you could remain in visual contact with a survivor on the ground or an infantryman under fire, long loiter times … these were all the characteristics of a good CAS or CSAR platform. The ageing A-1E Skyraider (above left and right) did all these things well, and the A-37A Dragonfly (below) was a diminutive jet-powered alternative that also had strengths. But a dedicated platform was needed, and the A-X programme sought to provide a solution. *(USAF)*

available in limited numbers and was vulnerable to anti-aircraft artillery (AAA) of both optical- and radar-guided varieties.

Much of the quandary in which the Air Force now found itself could be explained by its doctrinal propensities. The Air Force had strong leanings towards strategic bombing and air superiority, and CAS was so low on its list of mission sets that even battlefield air interdiction (BAI) – *ie* attacking the enemy behind the forward line of troops – was given greater importance. As might be expected, therefore, the Air Force built its fighters to be good at what it envisaged they'd be doing most, so that speed and survivability trumped loiter time and slow-speed handling. Moreover, the Air Force wanted to build fighter aircraft (aircraft designated with an 'F' prefix), not attack aircraft (denoted by an 'A' prefix). And so, with its hardware built in the form of high- and fast-flying fighters, the Air Force spent most of its time training its pilots in the art of air-to-air combat.

For the US Army, CAS doctrine was of supreme importance and the need for effective CAS grew more pressing with each passing day. On the battlefields of Vietnam, the Army was deploying troops rapidly using newly devised air mobility tactics, but time was of the essence: infantrymen were dying while the Air Force tried desperately to fill the capability gap. The Army could only look on as the Air Force fielded fighters that carried limited ordnance, offered small windows of time in which they could loiter, and were especially vulnerable to enemy ground fire when low and slow.

The experience was hugely frustrating for the Army, not least because the doctrine laid out for the armed services prohibited it from operating fixed-wing aircraft in the CAS role. Working around this, it re-roled UH-1 Huey 'Slick' troop-carrier helicopters, arming them with rockets and fixed machine guns on sponsons. This provided CAS as the assault force neared the landing zone, but it also represented the proverbial 'band aid on a sucking wound' solution. What was needed was government oversight.

By 1965 Congress had become aware of the CAS shortfall and the tension that existed between Air Force and Army. US Representative

ABOVE The US Army's AH-56A Cheyenne Advanced Aerial Fire Support System attack helicopter was intended to fill a void left by the Air Force's fast jets. It was a threat to the Air Force insofar as the Army developing rotary wing assets to conduct the CAS mission could have resulted in the Air Force losing the mission from its doctrinal statement altogether. *(US Army)*

Otis Pike chaired a subcommittee in the winter of 1965, castigating the Air Force when its report was published in early 1966 for failing to develop a CAS platform. Thus, in the weeks following the report's release, Army Chief of Staff General Harold Johnson and Air Force Chief of Staff General John McConnell met discreetly to try to resolve the matter directly.

The meeting of the two heads of service certainly laid to rest some historical contentions. The Army agreed to hand over its fixed-wing de Havilland Canada C-7 Caribou support assets to the Air Force, and the Air Force agreed that it would allow the continued use of helicopters in the escort and CAS role. To that end, the Air Force would not attempt to block the Army's continued development of the AH-56A Cheyenne Advanced Aerial Fire Support System attack helicopter, but it would expect it to compete for funding and approval with any direct-fire fixed-wing platforms that it might develop in the future.

However, the working agreement fell short of clearly articulating and defining who would do what in the race to develop a CAS capability, and consequently the Army and Air Force would each continue along its own path – whether that put them in competition with one another or not – in developing rotary- and fixed-wing assets, respectively.

ABOVE The F-111A Aardvark was fast and sophisticated, representing the sort of fighter in which the Air Force wanted to invest. It also formed part of the Air Force's concept of mixed force structures. A simple CAS platform would sit at the bottom of such a structure. *(USAF)*

With some of the doctrinal differences between the services nullified, revised tactical force structures could be deployed. A March 1965 force structure report recommended a mix of high-value F aircraft, including the F-4C and General Dynamics F-111A Aardvark, with a cheaper tactical platform that could deliver CAS, special air warfare and ground-attack missions, and prove survivable in the densely guarded low-altitude environs of North Vietnam.

In April 1965 the Air Force began to develop a low-cost multi-purpose fighter, the F-X, which could fill this capability gap. The Vought A-7 Corsair II, a Navy attack jet, was a prime candidate; so too was the Northrop F-5, a low-cost lightweight fighter being developed under the Military Assistance Program for some of America's less wealthy allies. The latter offered poor cost-effectiveness, and so by the winter of that year the Air Force was pursuing a custom variant of the Corsair – the A-7D.

Meanwhile, the Air Force was looking more closely at the Army's attempts to fill the CAS gap. An August 1966 study concluded that the Army was generally happier with the CAS that the Air Force was now supplying, but this statement was grossly misleading because the Army had by now firmly committed to filling the capability gap itself, wherever and whenever possible. To that end, helicopter gunships – including the new Cobra – presented the Air Force with something of a challenge to its authority.

To add to these woes, the D-model A-7 – which had been marketed as a low-cost platform at $1.5 million per aircraft and, importantly, one that could be developed and delivered to service quickly – was now the subject of delays and cost increases. Acquisition of the attack jet had begun in December 1965, and a contract to procure the A-7D was delivered in October 1966, but Tactical Air Command (TAC) specified changes that included the installation of a new engine and avionics. Together, these changes delayed the programme considerably (by 2–3 years) and drove the cost up ($3.4 million per aircraft in 1971).

It was fortuitous, then, that the Air Force's 1966 CAS study had also recommended the acquisition of a CAS platform that was even simpler than the A-7D, but more capable than

the A-1E Skyraider. On 8 September 1966, McConnell had directed his staff to design, develop, and deliver to service a dedicated CAS platform, leading to the December publication of a Requirements Action Directive (RAD) for the so-called A-X.

A-X concept studies

The A-X RAD encouraged the use of off-the-shelf technology as a way of getting the aircraft to IOC (Initial Operational Capability) as quickly as possible. There were two notable examples of this. Firstly, the engines; and, secondly, the avionics (communications, navigation and weapons delivery), which also had to be compatible with Air Force Forward Air Control (FAC) equipment and Army rotary-wing assets.

Broadly speaking, the A-X would be a CAS platform that would also provide escort for rotary-wing platforms and slower fixed-wing assets, and could be tasked to deliver armed reconnaissance and vehicle convoy protection. Its single pilot would enjoy all the benefits of a lightweight strike platform without having to endure compromises in maximum payload, low altitude handling and performance, or weapons delivery stability up to 400kt.

ABOVE A formation of LTV A-7Ds of the 354th Tactical Fighter Wing, over Myrtle Beach Air Force Base, South Carolina. The Corsair II was unceremoniously christened the SLUF (slow ugly fucker) by its pilots, indicating that it had all the credentials of an excellent CAS platform! *(USAF)*

Performance parameter	Desired	Required
Gross weight (lb)	22,500	30,000
Payload – mixed ordnance (lb)	8,000	6,000
Combat radius (nautical miles)	n/a	200
Loiter time @ combat radius (hr)	n/a	2
Minimum manoeuvring speed @ 5,000ft (kt)	120	150
Turn radius @ combat weight (ft)	1,000	2,000
Maximum speed @ sea level with external ordnance (kt)	550	450

Because the A-X would have to be able to navigate by night and in all weather, to include transoceanic ferry flights, its navigation equipment had to be compatible with existing and future conventional radio-navigation facilities. Based on Air Force and contractor studies, the estimated unit flyaway cost for the A-X was $1–$1.2 million (FY70$) depending on purchase quantities. Research and development costs were estimated at $240 million.

Once at the target the A-X would be able to employ internally mounted 20mm guns and conventional weapons hung on six ordnance stations. A limited air-to-air missile capability was specified, but only for use as a defensive measure. Further, the RAD listed an internally mounted recoilless rifle as a desirable feature. To sight and employ these weapons, an optical sight with a reticle that could be manually depressed was required. Ideally the A-X pilot would also benefit from an automatic release system fed an accurate slant range by an onboard ranging device, but that was a desirable feature, not a requirement.

With the ruggedness of the A-1E Skyraider impressing all those who flew or were supported by it, survivability was a key component of the RAD – the A-X would have to be tough. From the start, it would have to demonstrate inherent structural and system survivability. At the very least it had to have self-sealing fuel tanks and a manual backup system for any powered flight controls. In addition the pilot and critical systems would have to be protected from projectile strikes up to 14.5mm in calibre. To top it off, these systems could not be onerous to maintain or repair.

The Aeronautical Systems Division's F-X System Program Office (SPO) supervised the A-X programme, preparing a request for proposal (RFP) to industry for system studies in January 1967, then releasing it to McDonnell Douglas, Northrop, Grumman and General Dynamics in March. By September 1967 all four had responded, allowing the ASD to roll the designs and proposals into a Concept Formulation Package (CFP), the first iteration of which would come out in March 1968. In the interim, the ASD wrote a preliminary proposal outlining two potential A-X designs. They also provided a notional IOC date of 1970.

The first design was a single turbo-prop design, the second a twin wing-mounted turbofan design. Complementing the ASD proposal was data from the Air Force Armament

BELOW A Douglas A-1E prepares for another combat mission over South Vietnam. The Skyraider was noteworthy for the great number of weapons it could carry, as is evident here, and for its rugged nature. These were highly prized qualities in the CAS and CSAR mission sets. *(USAF)*

Laboratory (AFAL). This team specified that the aircraft should be able to haul seven Mk 117 750lb general purpose bombs and 1,000 rounds of ammunition on a prescribed mission profile. That profile included a climb to 5,000ft at optimum power setting and a cruise of 200nm at 250kt, followed by a loiter for two hours at 5,000ft. From there, the A-X had to be able to descend to sea level for 15 minutes of combat at 250–300kt, then return to base via a cruise at 5,000ft at optimum power. On landing, it had to have 20 minutes' worth of fuel remaining to loiter at sea level.

Such was the prescriptive nature of the A-X's performance, and wing loading calculations were a topic of constant conversation. In their authoritative history of the A-10 programme, Doctors David Jacques and Dennis Strouble state: 'The vehicle design analysis investigated the parameters of wing loading (W/S) and aspect ratio and their relation to the major design requirements. The gross weights to accomplish the design mission were calculated for fixed values of aspect ratio and wing loading. The results indicated that "for a given wing loading, lower aspect ratios, in spite of greater induced drag during the mission, result in smaller vehicles. This is directly the result of lower wing weights based on the design factor." Other performance requirements considered included low speed manoeuvrability, cruise speed, take-off distance, and ferry range with and without external fuel tanks. The analysis led to a selected design point which could meet or exceed all requirements.'

With so much attention given to wing loading, of the SPO's two configurations the turboprop-powered version seemed to look strongest on paper. The GE T64-16 turboshaft engine gave a minimum gross weight of 27,000lb, Jacques and Strouble write, and this was 'determined by the sustained 1.5 g turn requirement and "for an arbitrary upper aspect ratio of 7in". A design point with an aspect ratio of 7 and wing loading of 60 met or exceeded all requirements for the turboprop design. The turbofan design was based on the GE CF700-2c engine because "it was the only turbofan type available in the thrust class of interest for a twin-engine configuration". The sea level maximum thrust for this engine was 3,880lb resulting in an aircraft

gross weight of 28,800lb. Only limited data was provided for the turbofan design due to the poor performance predicted for that configuration. Specifically, poor fuel flow characteristics and inadequate thrust available from the turbofan engines resulted in aircraft performance not meeting requirements for loiter time, take-off distance, and low speed manoeuvrability.'

While AFAL prescribed the profile and weapons loadings that made the A-X design so sensitive to wing loading calculations, the lab was also offering views on two options for an internal gun. The gun was crucial to the A-X programme from the start – the dependability and capability of an internal gun would offset clear limitations in the then-nascent development of air-to-ground missiles.

The first option took a modified 20mm M61 Vulcan gun and modified it to fire a 30mm round that had lower muzzle velocity and correspondingly lower recoil. While this gun was attractive for its six-barrel configuration and a rate of fire up to 6,000 rounds per minute, it was also attractive because its technology was achievable in the near term. By contrast, the second option – for a 25mm gun with higher muzzle velocity (for improved stand-off) – could only be delivered in 1972, two years outside the A-X IOC schedule as it then stood.

Another component that could add significant weight – and capability – was the avionics suite carried by the aircraft. ASD's proposal catered for three levels of avionics sophistication: a 'skeleton' avionics package that delivered basic communication and visual

ABOVE Maintainers work on the gun barrel of the 20mm M61A1 Vulcan gun. It was this weapon that was the focus of initial interest for the A-X programme, but it soon became clear that, while a safe bet, the CAS mission demanded something with greater effectiveness against the latest Soviet armour. *(USAF)*

flight rules (VFR) navigation aids; a 'lean' package consisting of Doppler navigation, a radar ranger that could detect moving targets and a gun camera; and a third level that added support for the AGM-65 Maverick fire and forget missile (then in development). This third option was most popular because the Maverick was seen as a crucial weapon in the CAS role. And, with a cockpit-installed TV screen to show what the missile's IR (infrared) or EO (electro-optical) seeker could see, it also improved the A-X's potential in the armed reconnaissance role.

The concept formulation package

With the A-X proposal and the four contractor studies in place, the A-X working group delivered its Concept Formulation Package (CFP). By now, the proposed December 1970 IOC was looking too risky to bet on, so a six-month delay was introduced.

The CFP outlined three missions for the A-X in the Close Air Support domain: Close Support Fire (CSF), Armed Escort (AE), and Armed Reconnaissance (AR). It also highlighted the attendant qualities that would allow the A-X to execute these missions: responsiveness (the ability to operate from a forward operating base, among other things), lethality, survivability (from small arms, 7.62mm and 14.5mm machine guns, the Soviet ZSU-23mm system and IR and radar-guided missiles) and simplicity.

These characteristics were converted

into aircraft performance requirements. Responsiveness was defined by combat radius, minimum take-off distance, cruise speed and loiter time. Complexity would be measured in maintenance man-hours per flying hour (MMH/FH), which for contemporary fighters like the F-4 stood at 33.2, compared to the A-37's 14.3. Ongoing combat in South East Asia, in addition to historical analysis from Korea, informed the CFP's focus on survivability for pilot, engine(s), structural integrity and flight controls. This in turn drove planners to explicitly outline four areas in which the A-X should excel: the pilot had to be well protected; the engines should be shielded and made as redundant as possible; fuel had to be protected from ignition sources and fire; and manual flight controls had to be practically indestructible. High instantaneous and sustained g-limits, meanwhile, would ensure that the aircraft was manoeuvrable enough to operate in a contested low-altitude environment.

In order to get 50% of its weapons within a 100ft radius of the target (called the 'circular error probable', or CEP) on its first pass, the CFP determined that the A-X had to be stable at airspeeds across the 200–300kt range and at dive angles up to 50–70°.

All four contractors from the May 1967 study submitted design approaches to the Concept Formulation Package, but all were found wanting.

Meanwhile, the groundwork on the A-X's gun was well under way. In January 1968, nine months after the ASD's proposal had been delivered, Air Force leaders had approved the Requirements Action Directive for Air-to-Ground Gun Systems for Close Support Aircraft, specifying three target sets against which it should excel: troops in the open, under tree cover and in foxholes; tanks and armoured personnel carriers; and hardened targets such as bunkers. The Close Air Support Gun System Study Group of the Armament Laboratory had in the meantime commissioned its own studies into what should equip the A-X, and it would eventually publish its final report in September 1969, recommending a 30mm, internally mounted Gatling gun system and attendant depleted uranium rounds.

By June 1968 the Air Force was pushing the A-X programme towards contract definition

BELOW Marines from the 1st Marine Division, 3rd Amphibious Armored Vehicle Battalion, add realism to Exercise Kernel Blitz 97 by driving former Soviet bloc ZSU-23-4 AAA systems. It was this sort of system that the A-X was designed to contend with. *(US Marine Corps)*

ABOVE **The General Electric GAU-8/A displayed next to a Volkswagen Beetle for size comparison. The A-X programme was noteworthy for being run from the beginning to accommodate the gun, not the other way around.** *(USAF)*

stage. A Development Concept Paper (DCP) was submitted in December, but progress was so slow that the IOC for the A-X slipped to 1971. The delays stemmed from uncertainty about whether the A-X would be purchased instead of some of the A-7Ds, and whether the proposed A-X was too big, carried too much ordnance and was altogether over-specified. The result was that the Air Force reconvened the A-X Working Group to fully complete the CFP, and a slightly smaller, lighter and cheaper design was proposed.

On the plus side, Robert McNamara was by now no longer Defense Secretary, so the Air Force could reintroduce competitive prototyping (McNamara had outlawed this), even though this would cause the IOC to slip even further, to 1974. The delay benefited the engine manufacturers, including General Electric, which had continued to develop high-bypass turbofans.

Finally, on 10 April 1970, the A-X programme was authorised and the Special Program Office, which had until then been manned only by a skeleton staff, was fully manned.

Request for proposals

With the SPO now staffed at a level that allowed it to undertake complex work, an RFP could be issued and processed. The SPO ran not only the A-X programme (to include engine and avionics programmes), but also that of its internal gun, by now designated GAU-

8/A (see Chapter 7 for more about its history and the specifications of the Avenger). The RFP went out to 12 organisations in early May 1970, giving them three months to respond. In the event, only six did: Fairchild Hiller, Boeing, Northrop, Cessna, General Dynamics and Lockheed Aircraft.

At just 104 pages, the RFP was a metaphor for the aircraft for which it asked contractors to submit proposals: to the point and without frills. It focused on two primary goals – weapon system effectiveness and low cost, the latter of which was pegged at $1.4 million flyaway cost per aircraft (FY70 US dollars), assuming a 600 aircraft purchase. The RFP specified that, following a 75-day period for the Air Force to consider responses, two contractors would be taken to a fixed price Competitive Prototype Phase (CPP).

Of the six proposals, four specified the GE TF-34 turbofan engine as their power plant of choice, with a fifth opting for it as a backup. 'By 1970, the TF-34 was promising approximately 9,000lb of thrust,' wrote Jacques and Strouble, 'more than twice the thrust of the GE CF700 turbofan engine that was investigated during the early concept studies.'

By October 1970 the Air Force had evaluated the six proposals, including Boeing's lone recommendation for a turboprop-powered design – and Fairchild Hiller and Northrop were announced publicly as the shortlisted CPP contractors on 18 December 1970.

To build two prototypes for flight test and evaluation by the US Air Force, Northrop received $28.8 million, while Fairchild Hiller's Republic Division received $41.2 million. The difference in funding between the two is explained by the greater costs associated with Fairchild's selection of the TF-34, versus Northrop's selection of the Lycoming F102 engine (with TF-34 as backup). The Air Force designated the designs A-9A (Northrop) and A-10A (Fairchild), and the actual prototypes would feature a 'Y' prefix (YA-9A and YA-10A).

The contenders: Northrop A-9A and Fairchild A-10A

The A-9A exemplified the design-to-cost approach that had been impressed upon the contractors at the RFP stage – the Air Force had made it clear that if there was a choice between cost and performance, cost would win. Thus the Northrop design was powered by two non-afterburning YF102 engines, each rated at 7,500lb of static thrust, one located beneath each of the high-mounted wings. Because these cheaper engines also developed less thrust than the TF-34s installed on the competing A-10A design, an increased wingspan was needed to produce low-speed manoeuvrability, in keeping with the CAS mission. Northrop liberally took off-

THIS PAGE Northrop's YA-9 was a bruiser of a design, and looked the part for sure. It took the low-cost element of the A-X brief at face value, taking commercial and military off-the-shelf components to a new level: nose landing gear from the Northrop A-5 Vigilante, main landing gear components from the McDonnell Douglas A-4 Skyhawk, wheels and brakes from the Grumman Gulfstream 2, and the ubiquitous Douglas Escapac ejection seat. Like the YA-10, it was built with ample redundancy incorporated into its flight control and auxiliary systems, and it reduced the burden on the logistics supply chain by ensuring that parts for the left and right were as interchangeable as possible. Note the high wing, which would have made it easier to load weapons on to the wing pylons compared to the A-10's low wing. (USAF)

the-shelf components to further drive down costs, installing the nose landing gear from the Northrop A-5 Vigilante, main landing gear components from the McDonnell Douglas A-4 Skyhawk, wheels and brakes from the Grumman Gulfstream 2, and the ubiquitous Douglas Escapac ejection seat.

Offering more than just a nod to survivability, Northrop had gone as far as adding access doors that would blow out to release the overpressure of an internal explosion. Beneath the surface, the hydraulic flight controls with manual backup and redundancy were routed around a critical structure that also had redundancy built in. In the wings, self-sealing fuel tanks – each filled with foam – limited the chance of explosion. Finally, a 'bathtub' of armour plating wrapped around the cockpit.

The manufacture of interchangeable components for the flight controls, engines and wings – you could install the same control surface on either wing, for example – meant that not only were production costs reduced, but supportability of deployed aircraft would be similarly improved. Meanwhile, the installation of the engine at chest-height and the similarly elevated weapons attachment points made for an improved maintenance experience and an engine change in less than half an hour.

Fairchild's A-10A was much different to the A-9A. Twin turbofans were mounted in pods in an elevated position above the aircraft's empennage, the exhaust plumes from the two TF-34s nicely masked from the seeker

THIS PAGE Fairchild Republic YA-10A 71-1369 (top) was the first prototype built, and 370 (centre and bottom) was the second. The prototype YA-10s were later joined by six pre-production A-10s for flight tests and evaluations. Fairchild's high-mounted engine configuration is plain to see here, keeping the engines well above the ground to limit the possibility of foreign object ingestion on rough or unprepared airstrips, and shielding the exhaust efflux from heat-seeking missiles below and to the side of the jet. The design's low-mounted wing and fuselage offered 11 weapons stations. Here, two configurations are demonstrated: (centre) 22 x Mk 82 500lb bombs, and (bottom) 16 x Mk 82 and 2 x Mk 84 2,000lb bombs. *(USAF)*

heads of any ground-based IR missiles by a tail configuration that looked more at home on a World War Two bomber than it did on a 1970s attack aircraft. These design features ensured that the aircraft could not only operate from unprepared airstrips (where the engines would be less likely to suck up foreign objects), but could also easily 'hot' rearm and refuel – *ie* keeping the engines running while the aircraft was 'turned around' in rapid fashion.

In contrast to the A-9, the A-10's wing was low-set, and its wing-mounted landing gear offered a wider base. But, like the A-9,

Fairchild's offering featured a titanium bathtub, interchangeable parts, redundant and manual flight controls and extensive protection from explosion and fire.

Flight testing begins

The YA-10A (tail number 11369) made its first flight on 10 May 1972, while the YA-9A first flew a little over a week later. Between May and October 1972 Northrop accrued 162 hours of flight-testing the YA-9A, while Fairchild put 190 hours on the YA-10A.

Getting the GAU-8/A Avenger integrated into the A-10 as early as possible was a priority for the A-X programme office, but the gun was undergoing a separate tender process and was not instantly available. Seen installed here, it's easy to appreciate how the A-10 was designed to fit around the gun – every inch of space is carefully utilised, even to the point of displacing the nose landing gear to the right of the centreline. *(USAF)*

With contractor tests complete, the actual fly-off was conducted at Edwards AFB, California, between 10 October and 9 December. The competition saw 123 YA-9A sorties (146 flight hours) and 87 YA-10A sorties (138.5 flight hours), during which the M61 20mm Gatling Gun was fired (the GAU-8/A was not ready) and weapons delivery accuracy was tested.

The Air Force concluded that in most critical areas there was little to choose between the two designs. In fact, secondary considerations such as how well the designs handled on the ground, and which was most likely to be delivered on time, suddenly became much more important metrics to take note of.

On 28 February 1973, with the A-10A nudging ahead, and with the general consensus

LEFT The YA-9 seen on its maiden flight on 30 May 1972. Within a year or so it had become clear to the A-X test pilots that Fairchild's A-10 design had the edge. Noteworthy in this image is the way in which the main landing retracted into the engine nacelles. *(USAF)*

among the Air Force fly-off team being that Fairchild's design was the one they'd most confidently take to war, full-scale development of the A-10 was approved. On the same day the Air Force awarded GE a fixed-price, $28 million contract to develop and deliver 32 TF-34-100A engines.

Four months later GE would get another fixed-price contract for approximately $24 million when the Air Force announced it the winner of the GAU-8 competition. GE had competed for the contract against Philco Ford between January and early April. Hosted at Eglin AFB, Florida, the competition had been a walkover for GE, whose three prototypes fired 70,000 rounds compared to Philco Ford's meagre 16,000 rounds, the latter's prototypes being plagued by rounds jamming. Now victorious, GE was being paid to deliver seven pre-production gun assemblies and refurbish its three competition prototypes.

While the Air Force was more than satisfied with how the A-X programme was progressing, Congress was less convinced. As the summer of 1973 turned to autumn, it voiced concern that the A-10 offered limited bang per buck, and that there had to be a case for a fly-off between the A-10 and the A-7D, the latter of which was now in service and performing well over the skies of North and South Vietnam.

Naturally, the Air Force insisted that this was not necessary, but it was looking increasingly as though the only way to placate Congress was to do as they requested.

Meanwhile, by the end of 1972 the Army's AH-56A Cheyenne Advanced Aerial Fire Support System was dead in the water, and it was well on the way to specifying a new anti-armour helicopter (which would eventually become the AH-64 Apache).

Full-scale development

With Fairchild the winner of the A-X competition, the A-X SPO briefly became A-10 SPO, but was thereafter referred to formally as the 'Deputate for A-10'.

Among the Deputate's first responsibilities was planning and supporting the A-7D fly-off against the A-10. The fly-off ran between April and May 1974, when four seasoned Air Force pilots flew both types from McConnell AFB, Kansas, against simulated ground targets and air defences at Fort Riley, Kansas.

'The fly-off tested three aircraft configurations: heavy (12 Mk 82 500lb bombs), medium (6 Mk 82s) and clean,' report Jacques and Strouble. 'Bomb release as well as missile release and gun firing were simulated. Weather

ceilings simulated included unlimited, 5,000ft, 3,000ft, and 1,000ft. Each aircraft flew a total of 160 passes over the simulated battlefields. Data collected for the flights included Range Measurement System II, Cooper Harper (handling quality) ratings, and pilot summaries.'

The pilots, none of whom had previous A-7 or A-10 experience, expressed a preference for the A-7 only in scenarios where there was unlimited visibility; but when the weather closed in, the A-10 was a far better platform in which to rage around, flying CAS at low altitude over potential battlefields of Asia and Europe.

However, the political meddling didn't go away. When the Air Force published the fly-off findings, detractors of the A-10 simply shifted the focus elsewhere. Even after the A-10 entered production, politicians were lobbying to replace it. Some even believed that the Piper Enforcer – a modified P-51 Mustang with a turboprop engine – was a better choice than the A-10. It was, by any standard, a laughable suggestion when one considers the work the A-10 would be doing a decade or so later.

While the plan had originally been for the Air Force to fund ten pre-production A-10s, this was cut by four for budgetary reasons. The six pre-production aircraft were each allocated to specific test objectives:

73-1664 – performance and handling.
73-1665 – weapons certification.
73-1666 – subsystems and weapons delivery.
73-1667 – operational testing and evaluation.
73-1668 – Independent Initial Operational and Evaluation (IOT&E) and stores certification.
73-1669 – climate test.

Today, you can't think of the A-10 without instantly thinking of the GAU-8 too, but mating them was a significant engineering

ABOVE AND BELOW
Fairchild Republic A-10As on the flightline. They include development airframes 73-1667 and 73-1666 in the foreground, and prototypes 71-1369 and 71-1370 in darker grey and with striped pitot booms. *(USAF)*

Fairchild Republic A-10A 73-1667 (above) firing the 30mm Avenger. Secondary gun gas ignition (SGGI) from the GAU-8/A – a phenomenon whereby the cloud of gun exhaust gas around the nose ignites and starves the engines of oxygen – became a real concern to the A-10 community when a Hog was lost to it in June 1978 (the pilot ejected safely). Steps to resolve SGGI over the years included adding a gas scoop beneath the nose, changing the chemical mix of the 30mm-round propellant and adding a circuit that would cause the TF-34 ignition system to fire continuously when the gun trigger was depressed. *(USAF)*

achievement. The first phase in this process took place between December 1973 and January 1974, when the gun was installed and extensively ground tested. Next, a second gun was installed in a second A-10, and further ground tests conducted. Finally, Air Force pilots flew evaluation and operational tests to ensure that the marriage between gun and aircraft met the needs of wartime use.

Flight tests at Edwards AFB followed between February and March, revealing two things. Firstly, the gun produced a flame in front of the aircraft that obstructed forward vision and caused the engines to fluctuate as they ingested the gun's gasses (formally known as 'secondary gun gas ignition'); this was rectified by adding potassium nitrate to the ammunition propellant, which created a thick residue that clouded the front canopy and required the installation of a canopy washer. Secondly, the gun angle was too high for low-altitude and low-dive-angle strafing attacks. A 2° change in gun alignment resolved the matter.

Into production and service

In July 1974, plans for low-rate production of the A-10, GAU-8/A and attendant 30mm ammunition were created. The flight test programme had gone well, and while there were some concerns that Fairchild might

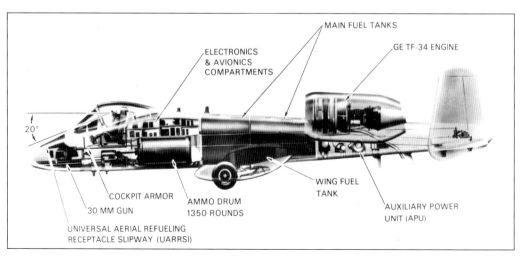

THIS PAGE Under construction at Fairchild Republic's Hagerstown, Maryland, plant, A-10 wing (top left) and fuselages assemblies (top right and right) are brought together. All 712 production A-10s were built at this site. *(USAF)*

fail to meet the 'design-to-cost' briefing that had characterised the A-X programme from the start, the A-10 Deputate's estimate of a $1.6-million flyaway cost (FY70$, 600 aircraft) was still within acceptable limits.

With the approval of the Secretary of the Air Force, the Air Force proceeded with initial A-10A production (52 airframes) at the end of July. Ongoing development test and evaluation (DT&E) at Edwards fed into the initial production design, and by the end of 1975 the final major test – fatigue testing – had been completed.

The first production A-10A flew on 10 October 1975. On 30 March the following year Tactical Air Command accepted the first production A-10, and two months later approval for full-rate production of the GAU-8/A was given.

The first USAF unit to fly the A-10 had been the 6510th Test Wing at the Air Force Flight Test Center, Edwards AFB – the squadron responsible for pre-service tests and trials, using prototype and pre-production aircraft. The 3246th Test Wing at Eglin AFB, Florida, had also flown the aircraft during armament trials.

The first operational A-10A was delivered – five months late, because of the reduction in flight test A-10 numbers from ten to six – to the 355th Tactical Training Wing (TTW) at Davis-Monthan Air Base, Tucson, Arizona. It was the start of an enduring relationship between the Wing and the A-10, and it was here that the pilots from the first A-10 combat wing – the 354th Tactical Fighter Wing (TFW) at Myrtle Beach Air Base, South Carolina – were trained as they transitioned to the new aircraft. They achieved full combat readiness in early 1978, sending their A-7Es off to other units in the process.

The next step in the introduction to service was the establishment of a training unit, the 355th Tactical Fighter Wing at Davis-Monthan AFB, which began trading-in Vought A-7s for A-10s in March 1976. The initial squadron was the 333rd Tactical Fighter Training Squadron 'Lancers', joined soon after by the 358th TFTS 'Lobos'.

The 354th Tactical Fighter Wing at Myrtle Beach was the first operational wing to trade-in A-7Es for A-10s, a process that began in late 1976. The Wing's 353rd, 355th and 356th Squadrons were instrumental in developing tactics, techniques and procedures to get the most from the new aircraft. This task was eventually taken over by the 57th Tactical Training Wing at Nellis AFB, Nevada, a dedicated operational test wing that began evaluating the A-10 in October 1977. Their work abutted the Air Force and Army's JAWS (Joint Attack Weapons System) trials, which defined the way A-10s would work with artillery and battlefield helicopters.

With US-based A-10 training, testing and operational units in place, it was time to begin equipping the most important A-10 wing of all: the 81st Tactical Fighter Wing, based on the east coast of England. It was the green plains of Germany's Fulda Gap that many believed would be the hunting grounds of the A-10 if the Cold War with Russia and her Eastern Bloc allies went 'hot', since Western intelligence knew that hundreds of Soviet tanks and armoured vehicles would pour into that vital space within

hours of war being declared. It would be the A-10's task to slow them. Consequently a large proportion of the A-10 force was earmarked for the 81st TFW. From the first aircraft arriving on 26 January 1979, the Wing built up to an impressive inventory of six squadrons (78th, 91st, 92nd, 509th, 510th and 511th TFS), accommodated at the twin bases of RAF Bentwaters and Woodbridge.

From Bentwaters and Woodbridge the Wing's A-10s would deploy to six Forward Operating Locations (FOLs) in West Germany, with each squadron being assigned a specific FOL. The FOLs were spread across both 2 ATAF (Allied Tactical Air Force) and 4 ATAF areas, and regular deployments allowed squadron pilots to familiarise themselves with the terrain in the areas they would be expected to defend in time of war. A-10 squadrons were primed to execute the anti-armour mission, and the pilots used their peacetime detachments to identify natural tank-killing grounds and potential vehicle choke points.

When the 100th A-10 was delivered the Air Force finally christened the jet Thunderbolt II, but those who flew and maintained it insisted on continuing the lineage of 'Hog' names that antecedents of the A-10 had been given (the F-105 was the Ultra Hog, the F-84F the Super Hog, and so on), and so the A-10 would forever be much better known as the Warthog, or simply Hog.

Early upgrades

With an increasing focus on theoretical A-10 operations in the Fulda Gap came corresponding changes in A-10 operator requirements. The A-10 was a stick-and-rudder aircraft, flown without computer input or assistance other than a simple Control And

BELOW Fairchild Republic A-10A 73-1665 in flight after the addition of the Pave Penny laser spot seeker system (seen here protruding below the pilot on the right side of the fuselage). The aircraft is carrying two GBU-10 laser-guided bombs. *(USAF)*

ABOVE The General Dynamics F-16 had everything going for it: it looked great, it was sophisticated, it was successful, and it was the child of the Fighter Mafia of the Pentagon. Realistically, it was never going to be the CAS or CSAR platform that the A-10 was, but that did not stop the A-10's ever-present detractors from proposing that the F-16 should replace Fairchild's outmoded and outdated design. *(USAF)*

Stability System (CAS) in the roll and pitch axis, which meant that it was tiring to operate in the threat-dense, weather-challenging and terrain-unaccommodating low-altitude environment of Europe. Dead reckoning and 'clock–map–ground' navigation was the norm, because the Hog had no INS (Inertial Navigation System), and weapons delivery against fleeting and evasive targets was frustrated by a simple heads-up display (HUD) and weapons-aiming computer. These things were all improved.

First came the AN/AAS-35(V) Pave Penny (1978), a 14.5kg podded laser spot tracker mounted on a vertical pylon flush to the right side of the forward fuselage. The pod allowed the A-10 pilot to detect the coded laser signal of a ground or airborne laser designator, displaying the laser spot as a diamond symbol in the HUD. This made it very easy for the A-10 pilot to see where the target was, and to deliver laser-guided weapons against ground targets designated for it by an airborne Forward Air Controller (FAC) or ground-based controller, or to engage the target under the diamond with the gun or any other munition.

Next, in 1980, came an INS, but it was no silver bullet and could do little more than guide the A-10 pilot to the rough vicinity (within a few miles) of his steer point. To this end, navigation remained a primary concern for the low-flying A-10 pilot. He came to rely on his ability to memorise the terrain, road layout and visual landmarks of his FOL, and to know by heart the geography of potential target areas if he was to have the spare capacity to then find and kill the enemy. On the plus side, a new HUD ensured that he received plenty of information about his navigation, flight and weapons status without having to peer down into the cockpit.

But as the A-10 was being incrementally

improved, production was about to cease: Congress had already voted in 1982 to halt all funding to the A-10. The Air Force's lightweight fighter, the General Dynamics F-16A, was in service and impressing observers with its credentials as a multi-role fighter. The tide of opinion was that the A-10 was looking less and less useful.

Naturally, Fairchild lobbied Congress to reconsider, and the Reagan Administration attempted to build consensus for purchase of another 50 A-10s through 1984, but these attempts were not successful.

So, with Fairchild unable to secure foreign buyers, it pushed the final A-10 off the assembly line in March 1984 – A-10A 712,[1] tail number 82-0665, ended 11 years of production. It was the last aircraft ever built at Fairchild's Hagerstown, Maryland, plant, and the end was also nigh for the company's aircraft business. By 1987 it had sold off its rights to the A-10 to Grumman, signalling the end of a 60-year association with aircraft that had started with the FC-1 in 1926.

---

1   Some sources claim that this was A-10 713, but only 712 production and pre-production A-10s were built. See appendix for full list of serials.

Reserve and ANG squadrons

Following the establishment of the 81st TFW, the European A-10 super unit at Bentwaters and Woodbridge, the Air Force turned its attention to swelling the ranks of US-based operators who could be called upon to reinforce the UK-based Hogs in the event of a European war.

Five Air National Guard squadrons (103rd TFS/CT, 104th TFS/MA, 128th TFS/WI, 174th TFS/NY and 175th TFS/MD) were equipped with the type, beginning with the 103rd in May 1979. This was significant, as it represented the first time that an ANG unit had received new aircraft directly from the manufacturer, as opposed to having second-hand equipment cascaded from active duty units. In 1990 and

BELOW Carrying canisters of Mk 20 Rockeye cluster bombs, AGM-65D Maverick missiles, Pave Penny and two AIM-9 Sidewinder air-to-air missiles, an A-10A flies over a target area during Operation Desert Storm, 1991. When the Hog finally got to run free in a combat environment, it secured a reprieve from impending retirement, dramatically silencing those critics that had for years denigrated it as a waste of time. *(USAF)*

1991 two more ANG units began flying the A-10A (110th TFS/MI and 111th TFS/PA), which was by now also referred to as the OA-10A (see Chapter 2) on account of a new Forward Air Control mission set that the small number of A-10 squadrons tasked them to provide.

Air Force Reserve units had begun to receive their A-10s in the 1980s, beginning with the 917th TFW in October 1980. Other AFRes units included the 442nd TFW, 926th TFW and 930th TFW.

More active-duty units were also formed in the early 1980s, consisting of the 23rd TFW at England AFB, Louisiana, as a second Stateside unit, plus the 51st and 343rd Composite Wings. The two latter were based in the Pacific region, the 51st in Korea and the 343rd in Alaska. Both received A-10s in the winter of 1981 to complete the initial deployment of the A-10 force.

The A-10 force disposition remained little changed for a decade, although in 1988 two squadrons of the 81st TFW split off to form the 10th TFW at RAF Alconbury – their operational task remained unchanged, however. In October 1987 the 602nd Air Control Wing at Davis-Monthan AFB began its adoption of the OA-10A in the FAC role.

Into combat and the road to the A-10C

The A-10 first saw combat in 1983, protecting US Marine Corps landings during Operation Urgent Fury (the United States' invasion of Grenada), but it was not until Operation Desert Storm in January 1991 that it would engage the enemy. See Chapter 4 for more about the A-10 in combat.

While the Hog performed with alacrity in the deserts of the Middle East – silencing its critics, stunning the rest of the world with its ability to kill armour, infantry and hardened fighting positions with ease, and earning it a reprieve from retirement – its limitations were well known and on the way to being addressed through the Low-Altitude Safety and Targeting Enhancement (LASTE) programme.

Delivered too late to make a difference to Hog drivers operating over Kuwait and Iraq, LASTE brought a radar altimeter, an autopilot and very accurate continuously calculated bomb impact predictions. The last comprised the so-called 'death dot' that allowed the pilot to place his targeting 'pipper' on the target, 'pickle' the weapon and know that he had a good chance of killing it.

An Enhanced Attitude Control (EAC) system was also installed, which allowed the pilot to put the gun pipper on the target, depress the trigger to its first stage and then relax his control of the stick as the aircraft then automatically held the pipper (in pitch) over the target, regardless of airspeed changes. When the range and sight picture looked good, he depressed the trigger to its second stage to fire the gun.

LASTE responded not only to desires to increase the A-10's lethality, but also, as the name suggests, the safety of pilots operating it in the low-altitude envelope. A-10s were flying into the ground during training, and in many instances this was the result of task saturation and a lack of terrain proximity warning. LASTE therefore added a Ground Collision Avoidance System (GCAS) to warn the pilot to pull up when collision with the terrain was imminent. LASTE also delivered NVG (night vision goggle) compatible cockpit lighting and covert external IR lighting that aided formation keeping by pilots on NVGs but was invisible to the human eye.

The upgrade was well received by the Hog community, but as the 1990s progressed and the A-10 went into combat against more-advanced opponents in the form of the Serbs, and in the less hospitable environments of the Balkans, it was clear that further high-tech investment was required.

An A-10 modernisation programme was duly proposed in 1997, leading to the 1999 installation of a GPS navigation system known as EGI (Embedded GPS-INS), and a cockpit control display unit (CDU) through which the pilot could access the EGI and navigation functions.

But these individual upgrades were too few to deliver a significant increase in capability. They were certainly the start of the A-10's march towards becoming more of a 'Gucci' jet, but what was actually needed was a far-reaching modification programme that truly brought the jet into the 21st century.

That programme came in the form of the 2001 A-10 Precision Engagement (PE) modification programme, and that in turn

resulted in the fabled A-10C (for a detailed discussion of the A-10C and other variants, see Chapter 2).

PE added a MIL-STD 1760 data bus (the computer channel through which the aircraft's navigation, weapons and targeting computers communicated), meaning that it would be capable of employing GPS-guided munitions and other precision guided weapons.

The man-machine interface was overhauled, and the cockpit received two 5in x 5in colour multifunction displays and HOTAS (hands-on throttle and stick) controllers from the F-16 (stick) and F-15E (right throttle). To make all this work, a new Integrated Flight and Fire Control Computer (IFFCC) was added, powering a programmable armament control set and digital stores management system (as opposed to the original switch-infested control panel).

Finally, a data link and the AAQ-28 Litening targeting pod were installed. The former gave the A-10C pilot the ability to share position, sensor and targeting information intraflight, and to receive and share targeting data with ground controllers. The latter allowed him to independently find, fix, target, track and engage the enemy with any of the A-10's weapons, but the laser-guided bomb (LGB) and joint direct attack munitions (JDAM) in particular.

While the PE programme was ultimately a huge success, it was slow in being delivered. The first flight of an A-10C occurred in January 2005, and a contract for low-rate initial production of 72 upgraded A-10s followed in March. The first production A-10C was delivered to Baltimore Air National Guard in August 2006, the same month that a contract for full-rate production of 107 units was awarded.

ABOVE Munitions specialists from the 23rd Tactical Fighter Wing, England Air Force Base, Louisiana, load 30mm rounds of ammunition into an A-10A for its GAU-8/A Avenger cannon prior to a sortie in support of Operation Desert Storm. *(USAF)*

ABOVE AND OPPOSITE The A-10A cockpit (above) and A-10C cockpit (right) are both indicative of the eras in which they were designed and built. For a 1970s design the A-10A cockpit is ergonomically sound, with 'steam gauges' logically positioned, and a single TV monitor installed in the top right to allow the Maverick missile to relay its EO or IR picture to the pilot. Fast-forward to the 2000s, and the C-model cockpit now has two multifunction colour displays, an up-front controller below the HUD to allow the pilot to enter flight, navigation, communications and weapons data into a new central computer, a digital stores management system, and HOTAS controls. *(USAF)*

With various Active Duty, Reserve, and Air National Guard units by now deployed to support the 'global war on terror' in Afghanistan and Iraq, the promised capabilities of the PE modification were in great demand. In fact, so pressing was the need that the ANG – free of the bureaucracy of the Active Duty Air Force – rapidly installed a data link and target pod on their jets. In doing so, they developed the interim A-10A+.

The A-10C finally reached initial operating capability in August 2007 and has been busy in combat ever since. A total of 356 A-10As have been upgraded and the aircraft has since received the Sniper XR target pod, which includes mid-wave FLIR (forward-looking infrared), dual-mode laser, CCD-TV (charge-coupled device television), laser spot tracker and IR marker.

Service life and wing replacement programme – Hog Up

The A-10 was built for a service life of 8,000 hours, but following its stellar performance in Iraq in 1991 Congress approved its continued operation out to 2008. The Air Force projected that this would see most A-10s accrue around 12,000 hours' fatigue life. In addition, the

A-10C was developed to remain in service until 2028. In short, the A-10's structural integrity has required focus (and continued to do so) to ensure it can meet its proposed extended service life.

Two months prior to the A-10C reaching IOC, in June 2007, the Air Force awarded Boeing the contract to replace wing panels on 242 A-10s. The wing programme, which was part of the 'Hog Up' Aircraft Structural Integrity Program, was designed to deliver a fatigue life of 16,000 hours and ran between 2000 and 2012.

In October 2008 the Air Force grounded the first 250 A-10s on a temporary basis: cracks had been discovered in the landing gear trunnions, and these aircraft would need to go through 'Hog Up' – the replacement of the outer wing panels of 368 A-10s and the centre wing panels on 242 of those – before returning to flight. The first re-winged aircraft were delivered to the Air Force in February 2012.

Despite the recent completion of Hog Up, the Air Force must still regularly inspect and repair ageing A-10 wings. In 2015 the Air Force submitted an RFI (Request For Information) to identify potential sources for production of additional new wing assemblies to support operational requirements through 2021. Were the Air Force to award a contract for a second round of new wing panels, it would reduce the wing maintenance and inspection overheads that are currently in place for the A-10 fleet.

Retirement looming

The A-10 has lived its entire life under threat of retirement or cancellation. From the earliest days of the A-X programme to today,

BELOW The A-10's straight wing is evident here. Tough, robust and laden with 11 hardpoints carrying a myriad of stores, the wing is subjected to extensive low-altitude manoeuvring. This, combined with the need to extend the number of fatigue life hours to 16,000, has led to the Hog Up programme. *(USAF)*

there has always been a force lobbying to send the Hog to the boneyard.

Throughout 2015 and 2016 the Air Force's desire to retire the A-10 led some to question its commitment to the CAS mission, invoking memories of the A-X programme's historical roots. The entire discussion is emotive and hotly debated, not least because the Hog's intended replacement – the Lockheed Martin F-35A Lightning II – is so controversial itself. Will retiring the A-10 leave a capability gap? Yes. Is that gap a priority to fill? It depends on who you ask.

There are, broadly speaking, two schools of thought: those who believe that the Air Force should retain the A-10 on the basis that the F-35 simply cannot perform 'Afghanistan style' CAS; and those who believe that in the 'next war' the threat environment will be so dense that the A-10 won't be able to survive. In short, the A-10 might be the best platform in a permissive environment, but against a capable opponent in a sophisticated air defence environment, only the F-35 would be able to survive. The Air Force argues that it would like both platforms in service, but that the budget cuts of two successive Obama administrations have forced it to take tough decisions. Only time – and the involvement of the United States in the conflicts of tomorrow – will tell whether those decisions were the correct ones.

At the time of writing (late 2016), the Air Force's official position was that the A-10 will be retired in 2019, to be replaced by F-16s. But some are pushing to keep the A-10 in service until at least 2022. The impetus for this stay in execution? Fighting Islamic State militants in Syria and Iraq, the A-10 has once again proved its worth and secured a reprieve through its actions in combat.

BELOW **The sun continually threatens to set on the A-10 – it has spent its life in a sort of permanent twilight zone where its retirement is constantly under review – but each time it seems that the end is finally here, an extension of service life or review of the capabilities it delivers comes to its rescue.** *(USAF)*

Chapter Two

A-10 Warthog variant briefing

It is remarkable that over a 40-year service life there have only been two major operational variants of the A-10, a fact that speaks volumes for the efficacy of the original design. This chapter provides a brief history of the A-10's operational development, focusing primarily on the technical aspects of that journey.

OPPOSITE Two A-10C Thunderbolt II aircraft fly a flight training mission in March 2010. The main visual differences between the A-10A, A-10A+ and A-10C are the addition of the GPS antenna and satellite radio antenna on the fuselage spine, aft of the canopy. *(USAF)*

LEFT, BELOW AND OPPOSITE TOP Test pilot Howard W. Nelson (left) was one of those who flew the YA-10A (below and right) during the evaluation and test programmes. Tragically, Nelson would die demonstrating the A-10A (#75-0294) at the 1977 Paris air show, grazing the ground while exiting a loop, resulting in the catastrophic failure of the tail section. Note the somewhat sharp edges of the vertical stabilisers in comparison to the production A-10A. *(USAF)*

YA-10A

Two YA-10s and six pre-production A-10s were built for the April to May 1973 comparative evaluation between the A-10 and A-7D Corsair II. The pre-production A-10s differed from the YA-10s most obviously in the detail of the wing design: leading edge slats were added to improve airflow to engines at higher angles of attack, the wingspan was increased, trailing edge fairings were added and the maximum travel of the Fowler flaps was decreased.

Other obvious changes included reshaping the vertical stabilisers, the installation of an in-flight refuelling receptacle in the nose, and the addition of a pylon on the front right of the nose to carry the Pave Penny laser spot tracker. Less obvious was the addition of an integrated boarding ladder and the reduction of the GAU-8A Avenger boresight by 2° to improve the ability to engage targets at short slant ranges.

A-10A

The first production A-10A flew on 10 October 1975. When production ended in 1984, 712 had been produced.

The A-10A was incrementally improved through the addition of an INS (Inertial Navigation System), AN/AAS-35(V) Pave Penny and a new HUD that was tied to the aircraft's

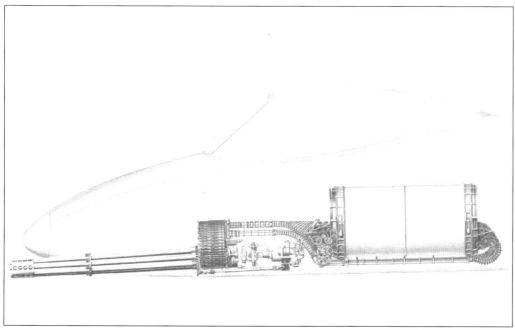

LEFT General Electric GAU-8/A side-view drawing, showing approximate location of the gun when installed in the YA-10A. *(USAF)*

ABOVE A-10A (73-1669) with Arctic Red markings flying out of Eielson Air Force Base, Alaska, on 2 March 1977. *(USAF)*

BELOW A-10A (76-518) was the 65th A-10 built. It is seen here in the markings of the 356th Tactical Fighter Squadron, 354th Tactical Fighter Wing, Myrtle Beach AFB, South Carolina, on 7 November 1977. *(USAF)*

systems to provide enhanced navigation, flight and weapons status.

Later came the Low-Altitude Safety and Targeting Enhancement (LASTE) programme. LASTE introduced a radar altimeter, NVG-compatible cockpit lighting, an autopilot with basic heading, pitch and altitude modes and the Enhanced Attitude Control system described in Chapter 1. In addition it featured a Ground Collision Avoidance System (GCAS). Externally, covert external IR lighting was installed.

An A-10A modernisation programme led to the 1999 installation of an Embedded GPS-INS (recognisable by the GPS dome antenna behind the canopy) and a control display unit located on the right-side cockpit console. The CDU is used to access EGI and navigation-related functions.

YA-10B Night/Adverse Weather

Ever keen to increase the sales potential of the A-10, Fairchild converted the first pre-production A-10A (73-1664) into a night-attack, all-weather version. The resultant designation was the YA-10B Night/Adverse Weather (N/AW).

The YA-10B was readily identifiable by the addition of a second crew station, with the pilot in the front seat and a weapons system officer seated behind him. The WSO would have had a forward-looking infrared (FLIR) pod mounted on the right side of the fuselage and a ground-mapping radar mounted on the left side. He would have been responsible for navigation, target acquisition and defensive countermeasures. To provide additional lateral stability, the YA-10B featured extended vertical stabilisers.

Flight-testing ran through 1979, but the Air Force was not interested in buying the design and the sole example was retired from flight-test service.

A-10A+

The A-10A+ (A-10 'Plus') was an interim designation used from 2006 by Air National Guard and Air Force Reserve units to describe A-10As that had some, but not all, components of the Precision Engagement (PE) update then being installed. The PE programme led to the A-10C.

The 'Plus' programme was conceived in 2002 when A-10 weapons officers were planning the A-10A's involvement in the forthcoming March 2003 Operation Iraqi Freedom. Realising that they needed, at the very least, to have some kind of target pod on the jet, and knowing that the PE programme

was going to be slow to arrive, they exercised their independence from the Active Duty Air Force and took matters into their own hands.

The A-10+ features colour displays and attendant moving map, and a basic integration of SADL (situational awareness data link) – a radio set that allows data transfer between the A-10 and ground forces – from 2007. Complementing SADL is the integration of the AAQ-28 Litening target pod to allow autonomous combat operations at night and in all weathers.

Following flight-testing in late 2007, around 100 A-10As were modified to A-10A+ standard from 2008 onwards. The first units to receive the A-10A+ were the 124th FW, Idaho ANG, 111th FW, Pennsylvania ANG, and the 917th Fighter Group, AFRes.

Within a year of first flight, A-10A+s were in combat in Western Iraq.

A-10C

The 2001 Precision Engagement programme led eventually to the A-10C. In August 2006, the 175th FW, Maryland ANG, and 110th FW, Michigan ANG, became the first units to receive the C-model Hog.

The A-10C boasts fully integrated SADL (as opposed to the A-10A+'s partial integration), linking the radio to the new Integrated Flight and Fire Control Computer (IFFCC) and, by extension, the HUD. In addition it enjoys ROVER (Remote Operational Video Enhanced Receiver) video-feed capability, allowing the pilot to slave the Litening pod's sensors to a SADL target or to independently fix a target, and then transmit the picture to a ground commander.

Crucially, the A-10C features the Digital Stores Management System (DSMS) missing from the 'Plus', enabling the jet to deliver Joint Direct Attack Munition (JDAM) and Wind-Corrected Munitions Dispenser (WCMD) stores.

IOC was declared in August 2007. The first combat employment of a JDAM by the A-10 came in September 2007, only three months after the first-ever drop during test and evaluation.

Some 356 A-10As were upgraded to become A-10Cs.

A/OA-10 and OA-10

In the early 1980s the Air Force introduced the OA-10A designation, signalling that it intended to use the A-10 in observation and FAC roles in addition to its attack role. This decision saw the inclusion of an INS and compatibility with 'Willie Pete' phosphorus marker rockets.

Later, in the 1990s, the USAF introduced additional designations for the A-10A, this time designed to reflect the primary mission that the

squadron operating it was tasked to execute – and, by extension, the qualifications of the pilots flying it – as opposed to distinguishing between aircraft capabilities.

This nomenclature – A-10A, OA-10 and A/OA-10 – can cause confusion, but the terms all refer to the same aircraft. A-10 typically identified aircraft of a squadron dedicated to the CAS mission, while OA-10 referred to one whose unit's tasking was weighted towards the airborne forward air controller (AFAC) mission. To seed further confusion, during Operation

ABOVE An A-10C Thunderbolt II from Eglin Air Force Base flies along the coast of Florida on 25 March 2010. The C-model Hog delivers an incredible punch and allows the pilot to operate in coordination with, but with significant independence from, a wide array of other forces in the battlespace. This helps to shorten the A-10's kill chain, and that's an important consideration in the CAS mission. *(USAF)*

Allied Force (see Chapter 4) Warthog squadrons were tasked with three missions – CAS, AFAC and combat search and rescue (CSAR), leading to the combined designation A/OA-10.

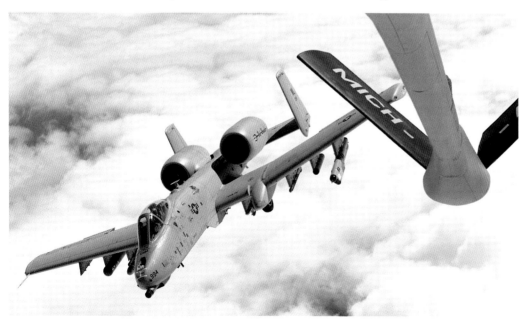

LEFT An A-10C departs after completing air-to-air refuelling from a KC135 Stratotanker while over Michigan, 13 September 2013. Both units are assigned to the Michigan Air National Guard and stationed at Selfridge Air National Guard Base. The A-10 is assigned to the 107th Fighter Squadron and the KC-135 is assigned to the 171st Air Refueling Squadron. *(USAF)*

Chapter Three

A-10 operators

The A-10 has only ever been operated by the United States Air Force, although Fairchild certainly attempted to sell the aircraft to a wider, international audience. Today, Hog squadrons exist in a handful of the major commands of the Active Duty Air Force and in the Air National Guard and the Air Force Reserve Command. The shifting sands of geopolitics mean that it is no longer operated by what was once its prime major command, United States Air Forces Europe.

OPPOSITE A 188th Fighter Wing A-10C releases a flare for the camera ship. The Wing undertook multiple deployments to Afghanistan with the A-10 Thunderbolt II, and regularly conducted training with joint terminal attack controllers from different branches of service to sharpen its close air support. In June 2014 the unit converted to the MQ-9 Reaper drone. *(USAF)*

A-10 squadrons span the states of Maryland, Michigan, Indiana and Idaho.

The reduction of A-10 squadrons started in the early 1990s, not because the aircraft was no longer needed – Operation Desert Storm had proven the opposite – but because the Cold War was over. One of the biggest changes was the dismantling of the vast USAFE force, leaving just one A-10 squadron based at the 52nd FW, Spangdahlem AB, Germany. This unit, the 81st FS, went on to see considerable action over Bosnia. Elsewhere, the Continental United States force was reduced to just one active-duty unit (355th Wing) and several ANG/AFRes units. In Alaska the former 343rd TFW (now 354th FW) operated a squadron of aircraft until its eventual deactivation (2007), while the 21st FS, 51st FW, remained in Korea.

Throughout the 2000s, the Base Realignment and Closure (BRAC) programme has further culled the number of A-10 operators. Today, in late 2016, all but one of the final 15 A-10 squadrons are based in the Continental US. That one exception is the 25th FS, found at Osan Air Base, Korea, where the A-10 forms the first line of defence against any would-be North Korean advance south of the demilitarised zone. USAFE's 81st FS was inactivated in 2013, marking the end of the A-10's permanent basing in Europe.

Air Force Materiel Command, which is

ABOVE Formation of Fairchild Republic A-10As of the 333rd TFTS, Davis-Monthan Air Force Base, Arizona, in January 1977. The closest two aircraft are S/N 75-268 and 75-270. *(USAF)*

The Active Duty component provides front-line squadrons in addition to a test and evaluation squadron (422nd TES, a squadron that also operates the F-15C, F-15E, F-16C, F-22 and F-35A) and a Weapons School unit (66th WS). Davis-Monthan Air Base, Arizona – the original home of the A-10 – today hosts both AD and AFRC A-10 squadrons, as does Moody AFB, Georgia. The Air National Guard's four

BELOW A-10Cs land in formation at Osan AB, South Korea. The base is home to the 25th FS, 51st FW. The squadron motto, 'Pilsung!', means 'Attack!' *(USAF)*

RIGHT An 81st FS, 52nd FW, A-10A peels away from the camera ship. The squadron, which had been stationed at Spangdahlem AB, Germany, was deactivated in June 2013, ending the A-10's presence in Europe. *(Steve Davies/FJPhotography.com)*

responsible for depot-level maintenance of the Hog, reported in October 2016 that 283 A-10s remain in operational service.

Current operators

Active Duty

- 25th Fighter Squadron (Osan Air Base, South Korea).
- 66th Weapons Squadron (Nellis Air Force Base, Nevada).
- 74th Fighter Squadron (Moody Air Force Base, Georgia).
- 75th Fighter Squadron (Moody Air Force Base, Georgia).

RIGHT An A-10C sits on the flightline before a training mission, 24 February 2011. The aircraft belongs to the 107th FS, 110th FW, Kellog Airport, Michigan Air National Guard, a unit that operated the Viper in combat in the Balkans, Afghanistan and Iraq before converting to the A-10 in May 2009. *(USAF)*

LEFT The 66th WPS markings on the tail identify this as a Weapons School A-10C. Based at Nellis AFB, Nevada. The school takes promising A-10 pilots and turns them into experts in both their own weapons system and tactics and those of the battlefield threats they may one day face. Here, two maintainers prepare a captive-carry AIM-9 Sidewinder for loading. *(USAF)*

ABOVE Four A-10s from the 111th Fighter Wing, Willow Grove Air Reserve Station, Pennsylvania, fly in formation after taking on fuel from a KC-10A Extender in May 2005. The unit was a long-standing A-10 operator, having replaced its A-37As with the A-10A in 1988, but following a 2013 announcement it has since converted to the MQ-9 Reaper. *(USAF)*

BELOW Selfridge's Red Devils are the 107th FS. Just visible here on the top right of the image is the open clamshell-type speedbrakes. Controlled by a switch on the throttle, the pilot can control the extent to which the speedbrakes open – when cracked open just a few degrees they increase the A-10's roll rate appreciably. *(USAF)*

- 354th Fighter Squadron (Davis-Monthan Air Force Base, Arizona).
- 357th Fighter Squadron (Davis-Monthan Air Force Base, Arizona).
- 422nd Test and Evaluation Squadron (Nellis Air Force Base, Nevada).

Air Force Reserve Command
- 45th Fighter Squadron (Davis-Monthan Air Force Base, Arizona).
- 47th Fighter Squadron (Davis-Monthan Air Force Base, Arizona).
- 76th Fighter Squadron (Moody Air Force Base, Georgia).
- 303rd Fighter Squadron (Whiteman Air Force Base, Missouri).

Air National Guard
- 104th Fighter Squadron (Warfield Air National Guard Base, Maryland).
- 107th Fighter Squadron (Selfridge Air National Guard Base, Michigan).
- 163rd Fighter Squadron (Fort Wayne Air National Guard Station, Indiana).
- 190th Fighter Squadron (Gowen Field Air National Guard Base, Idaho)

LEFT A 422nd Fighter Wing A-10C sits waiting for its next mission, intake covers installed to prevent birds or any other kind of foreign object from entering the big turbofans while the aircraft sits dormant. The Wing is an Air Force Reserve unit and is based at Whiteman AFB, Missouri. *(USAF)*

Historical operators

Active Duty
- 18th Tactical Fighter Squadron.
- 40th Flight Test Squadron.
- 55th Tactical Fighter Squadron.
- 78th Tactical Fighter Squadron.
- 81st Fighter Squadron.
- 91st Tactical Fighter Squadron.
- 92nd Tactical Fighter Squadron.
- 343rd Tactical Fighter Squadron.
- 353rd Tactical Fighter Squadron.
- 355th Tactical Fighter Squadron.
- 356th Tactical Fighter Squadron.
- 358th Fighter Squadron.
- 509th Tactical Fighter Squadron.
- 510th Tactical Fighter Squadron.
- 511th Tactical Fighter Squadron.

Air Force Reserve Command
- 706th Fighter Squadron.

Air National Guard
- 103rd Fighter Squadron.
- 118th Fighter Squadron.
- 131st Fighter Squadron.

- 138th Fighter Squadron.
- 172nd Fighter Squadron.
- 176th Tactical Fighter Squadron.
- 184th Fighter Squadron.

BELOW An A-10C of the 40th Flight Test Squadron flies over the Florida coast during a test sortie. The squadron is responsible for testing and evaluating new hardware and software before passing it on to the operational test squadron (422nd TES, Nellis AFB) for tactics development. *(USAF)*

Chapter Four

The A-10 at war

There's a common saying in the fighter business that if it looks great, it'll fly great. The A-10 is no oil painting, but its pilots love it regardless – looks be damned. Over the course of two and a half decades, the A-10 has been to war and, as the Americans say, opened a can of whoop ass on all those unfortunate enough to have been on the other side. There can be few other examples in history of a tactical fighter that has so readily adapted to different battlespaces and flexed so capably to meet the advances and needs of the modern day war-fighter.

OPPOSITE The A-10's formidable reputation in conflict zones around the world owes much to the GAU-8/A Avenger. Spewing 30mm shells, the Avenger has its own distinctive 'brrrrrrrt!' sound, delighting the ears of friendly forces on the ground almost as much as sight of the rounds hitting home. Of course, ground forces will see the rounds impact well before the sound of the gun reaches their ears. *(USAF)*

The A-10's introduction to combat came during Operation Urgent Fury, the US invasion of Grenada in October 1983. In a conflict that lasted only a matter of days, Hogs of the 23rd Tactical Fighter Wing staged out of Bridgetown, Barbados, to provide cover as US Marines landed on the Cariacou Islands. In the event, the landings went without contest and the Warthogs' tusks remained unbloodied.

Seven years later, in 1990, the dearth of combat experience was about to change dramatically. When Saddam Hussein, the dictator of Iraq, ordered his elite Republican Guard to roll south and take the tiny Gulf state of Kuwait, he poked a hornet's nest. Within a week the United States had deployed combat forces to the region to stave off any further aggression towards oil-rich Saudi Arabia, and in the months that followed a colossal build-up of American, British, French and other Coalition air, sea and land forces took place. Among them was the A-10 – clutched from the jaws of retirement, and about to prove itself incontestably the best close air support, combat search and rescue and tank-busting platform in the world.

Since then the A-10 has delivered

BELOW An A-10A Thunderbolt II aircraft takes part in a mission during Operation Desert Storm. It is armed with AIM-9 Sidewinder missiles, AGM-65 Maverick missiles and Mk 82 500lb bombs. (USAF)

capabilities to battlefield commanders in the Balkans (1990s), Afghanistan (2001 onwards), the second Gulf War (2003 onwards), Libya (2011) and Syria (2014 onwards).

Iraq – Operation Desert Storm

For Desert Storm, A-10As deployed to the Middle East were under the command of the US Central Command's 14th Air Division. In all, seven A-10 squadrons were assigned to the 354th TFW (Provisional), which constituted a monster Hog unit numbering 131 aircraft from one European and multiple US squadrons.

The first units (353rd and 355th TFSs of Myrtle Beach, Florida; 511th TFS, RAF Alconbury, England; and 706th TFS, Louisiana ANG), each with 24 aircraft, arrived at King Fahd International Airport, Saudi Arabia, on 15 August 1990. Then followed 48 A-10As of the 74th and 76th TFSs, England AFB, Louisiana, and 12 OA-10As of the 23rd Tactical Air Support Squadron, Davis-Monthan AFB, Arizona.

After months of build-up and planning, in the small hours of 17 January 1991 the US-led

RIGHT The pilot of an A-10A Thunderbolt II attack aircraft from the 23rd Tactical Fighter Wing of England AFB, Louisiana, communicates with his crew chief following a mission during Operation Desert Storm. *(USAF)*

Coalition pushed north from its bases across Saudi Arabia and other Gulf states, and into both Kuwait and Iraq. Operation Desert Storm was under way.

ODS was, as any good military campaign should be, defined by phases and stages. Three phases were executed in close chronological proximity. The first and second phases took out strategic targets. Coalition strike aircraft engaged integrated air defence system (IADS) nodes, military and auxiliary airfields, nodes used by command and control systems, sites suspected to house NBC weapons, and electrical power plants. In those few hours, Iraq's leadership and military were simultaneously deafened, blinded and hamstrung. As daybreak fell, phase three was ready to execute: both regular and elite Iraqi Army ground forces in Kuwait would now be pummelled ahead of a Coalition ground offensive.

Of all the ODS strike missions, 75% focused on ground forces in Kuwait. This comprised an estimated 5,000 defence elements – dug-in T-72 main battle tanks, artillery and air defences (SA-6, SA-13 shoulder-launched IR missiles and AAA) – attached to three heavy regular divisions and seven elite Republican Guard divisions strung along the Kuwait–Iraq border. Clearly, this wasn't a job for the faint-hearted.

Commanders tasked the medium- and high-altitude F-16 and B-52 strike aircraft to

BELOW A 355th TFS A-10A leaves the tanker during an ODS sortie. The 'lizard green' European theatre camouflage is typical of A-10s of that era; only later would the two-tone grey arrive that is so familiar today. *(USAF)*

engage the Republican Guard using unguided munitions. To the A-10 went the job of rooting out the regular Iraqi divisions, which lacked the level of sophisticated and integrated air defence of Saddam's own Republican Guard. The SA-6 mobile surface-to-air missile was the most deadly Iraqi asset.

This division of tasks was a touch ironic. After all, the SA-6 was exactly the sort of system that A-10 pilots at the time were trained to counter, and they were well prepared for combat in a high-intensity environment that featured integrated air defence systems and massed armour. But it was a decision made at the very top, so there was no arguing the point.

Planners divided Kuwait and Iraq into a grid pattern of 'kill boxes' (30nm x 30nm squares), then assigned strikers to freely operate each kill box. The A-10 immediately enjoyed success in destroying dug-in armour, but the F-16s and B-52s were less effective.

While killing massed armour and providing close air support was the A-10's 'bread and butter' mission set, in the 1980s it had also inherited the Airborne FAC role from the outgoing OV-10 and OA-37. Squadrons that took on the tactical air support AFAC role did so to the exclusion of all else. This meant that they didn't carry out strike missions, or, often,

even carry offensive weaponry – typically just the gun and white phosphorous marker rockets. They flew their 'killer-scout' OA-10s light and agile, unencumbered by the high drag index of masses of ordnance. During ODS, the 23rd Tactical Air Support Squadron (TASS) was responsible for this mission.

Killer-scout sorties were typically flown single-ship by the 23rd TASS. The lone pilot would roam the kill boxes of southern Kuwait, find and mark targets, then call in his A-10A attack brethren to deliver the fatal blow. On one day, two A-10 pilots of the 76th TFS, 23rd TFW, claimed 23 tanks destroyed, 5 using the GAU-8/A and the remainder with AGM-65 Mavericks. The kills were claimed in three successive engagements (each interspersed with a landing and hot rearm/refuel at a forward operating location), starting with an OA-10-led interdiction of Iraqi tanks and ending with combat search and rescue (CSAR) to protect a downed Marine Corps AV-8B Harrier II pilot. It was a startling testimony to what an incredible machine the A-10A was, and just how skilled the Hog community had become.

On 24 February the Coalition launched its ground offensive. Four days later, on 27 February, A-10s were finally instructed to attack a Republican Guard armoured division.

RIGHT A ground crewman signals as the pilot of a 353rd Tactical Fighter Squadron A-10 Thunderbolt II aircraft brings his plane to a stop upon arrival in support of Operation Desert Shield. Note the twin 600-gallon fuel tanks on the inboard stations. *(USAF)*

For three days, 48 Warthogs – organised into six waves of eight-ship formations – engaged the division. Finally, the gloves were off.

The A-10 showed its ruggedness on many occasions during ODS. At low-altitude and low airspeed, it represented a juicy target to the well-equipped Iraqi Army, yet only seven were downed during the course of 8,100 sorties. Around 70 A-10s were damaged by enemy fire, according to the 2951st Combat Logistic Support Squadron website. The squadron, which was responsible for A-10 battle damage repair, states: 'Many of the damages were undocumented cases of relatively minor problems. Some were even caused by their own aircraft such as a bomb lanyard slapping a wing flap, or a bomb fragment flying up and embedding into its engine cowling. But most was caused by small arm[s] fire and surface to air missiles. We had put together "Quick Fix" teams to deal with all these damages. At first we would go out to the revetment the aircraft parked in after returning from a mission, and give it a quick once over inspection for any damage. However, with the large number of minor damages we were finding, this process soon turned into tertiary inspections performed out at EOR [end-of-runway] itself, which gave us time to radio ahead for a Quick Fix team to be waiting for the aircraft to park.'

It's noteworthy that the Gulf War Air Power Survey (the Air Force's review of Desert Storm) found that more than 50% of damaged A-10s returned to service within four hours – a figure in line with the original brief for the A-X, and a validation of how well the A-10 had been designed to facilitate repair and rapid turnaround.

While 70 damaged A-10s accounts for more than half of those deployed, it pales into insignificance with the punishing toll the Hogs took on the Iraqis. At the end of the war A-10 pilots claimed the destruction of 967 tanks, 926 artillery pieces, 1,306 trucks, 501 armoured personnel carriers, 28 command posts and two Mi-8 helicopters.[1] This was in addition to possible SCUD launcher kills, EW radar kills and suppression of enemy air defences.

The official Air Force history states that 'A-10s had a mission capable rate of 95.7% ... [and] launched 90% of the AGM-65 Maverick missiles fired in the conflict. This success is partly attributed to the burning oil wells that provided Iraqi tanks cover from advanced electronics and high-flying fighters such as the F-15 and F-16; however, the smoke proved

1   This is the official Air Force tally of kills 'claimed' during the conflict, but it does not make clear whether the two Mi-8s were airborne at the time of their demise. Officially, the A-10 has been credited with only one air-to-air kill. See Chopper Popper in the Appendix.

ABOVE Preserved at the National Museum of the United States Air Force, this A-10A carries the markings of the 353rd TFS, as worn during Operation Desert Storm. *(USAF)*

ABOVE The 355th TFS poses in front of one of their trusty steeds at the end of Operation Desert Storm. The aircraft is armed with a full combat load, including SUU-25 flare pods, AGM-65D Mavericks and Mk 20 Rockeye II anti-armour cluster bombs. *(USAF)*

ineffective cover from the trained eye of the attack pilot, armed with the mighty GAU-8 and its stable airborne platform.'

While (or perhaps because) the Coalition stopped short of going all the way to Baghdad, the 1990s represented only the first decade of US and Coalition involvement in combat in Iraq. Combat operations simmered throughout the 1990s, starting first with Operation Southern Watch (August 1992 to March 2003) 'to enforce Iraqi compliance of [no-fly zone and air defence] restrictions placed by the Coalition following Operation Desert Storm'. It soon included Operation Northern Watch (a similar exercise to control airspace in northern Iraq), and bubbled over dramatically during limited escalations such as Operation Desert Fox. The A-10 supported it all, deploying to the Middle East as part of the Air Expeditionary Forces concept for 90 days at a time.

Kosovo – Operation Allied Force

While A-10 squadrons deployed to the Middle East operated over a baked, barren desert to keep Saddam Hussein in check, in Europe the thunderclouds were broiling over verdant and mountainous former Yugoslavia. It was pretty much this environment that the A-10 community had trained to operate in for so many years: poor weather; rising and irregular terrain; and an opponent who was former-Warsaw Pact, motivated and both well-trained and well equipped.

Military intervention in the Balkans became a foregone conclusion when political and economic efforts made no impact on the Bosnian Serb programme of ethnic cleansing its population of Muslims. A UN peace-keeping force was formed in April 1992, and in the

RIGHT An A-10A takes off on a mission against targets in Yugoslavia. The A-10 and OA-10 Thunderbolt IIs were the first Air Force aircraft specially designed for close air support of ground forces. *(USAF)*

CENTRE US Air Force airmen position a bomb load truck as members of a weapons load crew prepare to attach an AGM-65 Maverick missile to the wing of an A-10A at Gioia del Colle, Italy, for a NATO Operation Allied Force mission on 12 April 1999. *(USAF)*

12 months that followed, NATO commenced operations in the skies of Bosnia.

Among the NATO force were the A-10s of the 81st FS, 52nd FW, Spangdahlem AB, Germany. The squadron deployed to Aviano AB, Italy, to provide support, and were recognised as the only deployed aircraft able to provide CAS and AFAC at night. LASTE and enhancements to night-vision lighting in the cockpit, as well as covert external lighting, were at the heart of this capability. Later, the Block 40 F-16CGs of Aviano's 31st FW would take over most of the AFAC taskings, and were arguably much better equipped to do so given their dedicated night-strike training, holographic HUD and LANTIRN night navigation and targeting suite.

Of course, with no friendly troops on the ground the call for CAS never came. However, civilians were regularly in close proximity to the enemy, leading the Hog pilots to adopt the same urgency and attach the same significance to these situations as they would a CAS situation.

Trouble in the region was never far away. In September 1995 the United States once again led an international Coalition force during the 11-day air campaign christened Operation Deliberate Force. Deliberate Force rained down destruction on Bosnian Serb troops, armour and support vehicles in the open, ultimately

RIGHT A Hog pilot discusses his aeroplane's performance with his crew chief at Aviano Air Base, Italy, after a mission against targets in the Federal Republic of Yugoslavia on 30 March 1999, during NATO Operation Allied Force. *(USAF)*

forcing Serbian president Slobodan Milošević to accept a political solution known as the Dayton Peace Accords.

For the A-10 community, the two-week operation marked the introduction of operational and doctrinal changes. Doctrinally, the distinction between being an OA-10A squadron responsible for AFAC or an A-10A squadron responsible for attack went away, and all A-10 squadrons could incorporate the AFAC role into their 'doc statement' from then on. At an operational level, tactics continued to evolve. Whereas the combat over Iraq and Kuwait in 1991 had been largely characterised by daytime, low-altitude missions in clear weather, operations in the Balkans were producing tactics development geared towards night-time, medium-altitude operations and operations in bad weather.

As the Millennium approached, unrest in Kosovo increased. Once again, the A-10 was called to combat, and once again 'Spang's' Hogs deployed to Aviano in the early part of 1999 in support of Operation Allied Force. The undertaking was not insignificant: the Serbian Third Army had 40,000 concealed troops in a Kosovan valley, and boasted hundreds of tanks, armoured personnel carriers and artillery pieces that had been scattered among the Kosovan population. The Army was well defended against air attack, although its Air Force was poorly equipped by Coalition standards.

By the time the combat operations began on 24 March, 15 A-10As were at the Italian base. While most of the very tightly controlled target set for Allied Force was fixed infrastructure and C2 (command and control) located in Kosovo, Montenegro and Serbia, it was not long before the A-10 came into its own. An A-10 pilot was the on-scene commander on night four when an F-117 stealth fighter was shot down near Belgrade. The A-10 'Sandy', as CSAR forces are called, 'tracked the survivor's location, coordinated the rescue effort, and provided cover for rescue helicopters during the ingress, survivor pickup, and egress of enemy territory', according to the USAF Air University paper, 'A-10s over Kosovo'.

With a muddled picture of the battlespace a certainty, the A-10's AFAC prowess was always going to be important to the outcome of the campaign. Now equipped with EGI and an improved communications suite, the A-10 would work with intelligence, surveillance and reconnaissance platforms such as the E-8 JSTAR to find targets of opportunity. As the fixed target set was whittled down in the first days, fielded Serbian forces became the focus. The 81st FS's pilots started flying AFAC sorties on 30 March, launching out of Aviano on missions that lasted up to seven hours. They were initially hampered by low cloud, but they found and destroyed a Serbian truck park on 6 April and made easy pickings of main battle tank and infantry convoys in the days that followed.

With an operating rhythm in place, a quick redeployment to Gioia del Colle Air Base in southern Italy allowed the A-10 pilots to shave an hour off their flight time to their target areas across the Adriatic. This took place on 11 April, but they maintained the pressure on their foe, and by now the Serbian Third Army was fighting for its life. In fact, demand for

OPPOSITE Two A-10As form up before dropping away from a tanker aircraft for a mission against targets in the Federal Republic of Yugoslavia on 22 April 1999, during NATO Operation Allied Force. The Warthogs, deployed to Aviano Air Base, Italy, are from the 81st Fighter Squadron, Spangdahlem Air Base, Germany. *(USAF)*

BELOW An Air Force crew chief walks the wing as he does a post-flight check of an A-10 Thunderbolt II at Aviano Air Base, Italy, after it was flown against targets in the Federal Republic of Yugoslavia on 30 March 1999, during NATO Operation Allied Force. The two live AIM-9M missiles are there for self-protection, although there were probably few Hog pilots not ready to take a shot at an unwitting MiG! *(USAF)*

AFAC was so great that the Air National Guard formed the 104th Expeditionary Operations Group and deployed to Trapani AB, Sicily. The AEG comprised the 15 A-10s, plus 3 more based at Taszar, Hungary, to provide dedicated CSAR support in the event of a Coalition shoot-down over Northern Serbia. All 18 jets were taken from the Idaho, Michigan and Massachusetts ANGs, and some were involved in the successful CSAR operation to recover a downed F-16 pilot, making it two for nil for the A-10 Sandy force. Later the force would provide Sandy cover for a downed Royal Navy Fleet Air Arm Sea Harrier pilot.

In the 78 days between 6 April and 9 June, A-10s flew more than 1,000 AFAC missions. Once more the A-10's ruggedness came into play – two were hit by SA-14s, but neither was downed.

Iraq and Afghanistan – Operations Iraqi Freedom and Enduring Freedom

The 'war on terror' began in Afghanistan on 7 October 2001 with attacks on Taliban and al-Qaeda targets. The operation was called Enduring Freedom (OEF). A direct response to the 11 September attacks in the United States, OEF was the start of a war on Islamic terrorism

ABOVE Maintainers of the 81st Fighter Squadron, Spangdahlem Air Base, Germany, perform safety checks on an A-10 Thunderbolt after its return from missions over Yugoslavia on 30 March 1999. The mountainous background acts as a clue that the squadron deployed to Aviano Air Base, Italy, when it was tasked with supporting Allied Force. *(USAF)*

BELOW An A-10A of the 706th FS 'Fighting Cajuns', AFRC, sits at a desolate Bagram Airfield, Afghanistan, early on in Operation Enduring Freedom. The squadron deployed to Afghanistan first in 2002. *(USAF)*

that, on 19 March 2003, expanded to include Iraq (Operation Iraqi Freedom) and which continues to this day.

For most A-10 squadrons, OEF might have ignited a fire in their bellies to kill the enemy, but the new Global War on Terror simply elevated their operational tempo – they'd been inking combat time in their logbooks since 1991. In fact, the first A-10 units to take part in OEF were already deployed, staging out of Al Jaber, Kuwait, in support of Operation Southern Watch even as the twin towers collapsed in New York. Those units were the 332nd AEG, a 'rainbow' unit comprised of aircraft and people from several Air National Guard units, and the 355th Fighter Wing.

While rainbow units – so called because they were made up of aircraft with different-coloured fin flashes – had served the A-10 community well in Allied Force, they became a staple sight in the coming decade of Air Expeditionary Force (AEF) rotations to Afghanistan and Iraq. And what a tempo that AEF roster set: it was relentless. The official 355th FW's history provides an example: '[The Wing] retuned to Afghanistan again in March 2002, and then supported Operation Iraqi Freedom in March 2003. In October 2003 and again in September 2005, the 354th Fighter Squadron

"Bulldogs" deployed on five-month deployments to Bagram Air Field in Afghanistan. ... While the 2003 deployment saw limited action, the Bulldogs employed over 22,000 rounds of 30mm during 130 troops-in-contact situations during the 2005 deployment. ... The 354th Fighter Squadron returned to Afghanistan in May 2007 for a six-month deployment. Again, they provided 24-hour presence and Close Air Support expertise to Coalition forces in support of Operation Enduring Freedom. During this period, insurgent activity level was the highest recorded to date in OEF. The Bulldogs employed an unprecedented number of munitions during this deployment – over 150,000 rounds of 30mm in support of over 400 troops-in-contact situations.'

For the A-10, Operation Anaconda – which took place in March 2002 – represented the first large-scale ground operation in 'AFG' that required direct combat support – until then, friendly troops on the ground had consisted mostly of small pockets of Special Forces troops, and the A-10 had been kept away from the action (F-16s and F-15Es provided support instead).

Anaconda required members of the 74th Expeditionary Fighter Squadron (EFS) to provide round-the-clock AFAC and CAS coverage for

ABOVE An A-10A of the 104th Expeditionary Fighter Squadron takes off from Bagram in March 2003. Coalition forces in Afghanistan had launched an offensive, dubbed Operation Valiant Strike, on 20 March, aimed at villages and cave complexes east of Kandahar in the Sami Ghar mountains. A-10 pilots provided close air support for Army forces. Note how lightly loaded the aircraft is – carrying only two rocket pods and two Mk 82s – on account of the hot and high conditions in which it had to operate in Afghanistan. *(USAF)*

RIGHT AND ABOVE Then-Captain Kim 'KC' Campbell inspects the damage to her A-10A following a MANPAD (man portable air defence) hit over Baghdad, Iraq. Campbell returned the aircraft using the Manual Reversion Control System (see Appendix). *(USAF)*

around 1,700 airlifted US troops and 1,000 more Afghan militia. While they operated mostly from Al Jaber, Kuwait, in the initial stages, a detachment deployed to the former Soviet base of Bagram Airfield on 23 March, activating the

BELOW The rear end of an SUU-25 flare canister, photographed prior to loading on an A-10C at Kandahar Airfield, Afghanistan. The SUU-25 is used to shoot LUU-19 illumination devices – it provides IR illumination for NVG-equipped aircraft and ground operators. *(USAF)*

455th Air Expeditionary Group in the process.

For Operation Southern Watch (OSW), the standard combat loadout (SCL) for A-10s had been devised for killing armour: CBU-87 anti-armour cluster bombs, IIR AGM-65D Mavericks, rockets, an ECM pod, an AIM-9 missile and the GAU-8/A loaded with 'combat mix' – five depleted uranium (DU) rounds for every armour-piercing incendiary round (API). But in Afghanistan, the target sets and associated weapons effects were quite different; in Gary Wetzel's book *A-10 Thunderbolt II Units of Operation Enduring Freedom*, Captain Scott Campbell is quoted as saying: 'The new target sets in Afghanistan were dismounted troops and technical vehicles – soft targets in air-to-ground parlance – so we didn't need the anti-armour SCL. We decided to swap the CBUs for Mk 82 500-lb bombs with airburst fuses, as the latter was going to maximise the kill radius against flesh and soft targets. We definitely wanted white WP rockets, so we elected to load three pods worth because it sounded like we were going to be doing CAS. We also loaded some IR flares – LUU-19s – and elected to keep our Mavericks, using the weapons' IIR as a poor man's FLIR. That was how we found targets at night in the A-model. Then we changed the

ammunition, replacing all the DU and API shells with a full load of high explosive [HE] rounds. We dropped the ECM pod and the AIM-9s as well. The first combat load for OEF was four Mk 82 airburst bombs, two IIR Mavericks, one SUU-25 canister containing LUU-19s, three rocket pods and HEI for the gun.'

Loaded with this revised SCL, the A-10 was immediately in the thick of it, providing emergency CAS in the dead of night, and striking targets as diverse as bunkers and mobile enemy mortar teams. The Mk 82 airburst weapons proved particularly devastating against people and soft vehicles in the ravines, canyons and valleys of the Afghan mountains, blasting loose shale into the air so that anything in its path was shredded.

But in the rarefied air of the Afghan mountains, energy management was a key concern to the power-limited A-10 pilot. The Hog's turbofans were great at low altitude but wheezed up high. Smooth flying was especially important to maintain energy during refuelling from tankers in the mid-20,000ft altitude band, but even then it was sometimes the case that a tanker would have to enter a gentle descent to allow the A-10 to stay on the boom.

As the conflict progressed, the A-10

community worked particularly closely with the AC-130U Gunship and E-8 JSTARs to find and engage Taliban and al-Qaeda fighters. They moved in small groups, were difficult to identify as combatants because of their civilian attire and knew the terrain well.

So great was the demand for the A-10 to provide CAS around the clock that five aircraft temporarily deployed to Jacobabad, Pakistan, to shorten their transit to and from the battlefield.

But there was a queue of Allied aircraft waiting to take out the Taliban and those it sought to protect. It often fell to the A-10 pilot to provide overall command and control of the immediate battlespace, managing both manned and unmanned aircraft, tasking them against targets and deconflicting their flight paths. The fact that one person in a single-seat aircraft could do this spoke volumes about the standards to which A-10 pilots were being trained, and just how far the A-10A had come as a result of iterative improvements.

When Anaconda concluded at the end of March 2002 the operating rhythm in Afghanistan slowed for the remainder of the year. A-10s occasionally engaged the enemy, usually under the guidance of a Joint Terminal Air Controller, or JTAC, operating with a special

ABOVE An A-10C of the South Korea-based 25th Fighter Squadron releases a flare to decoy any MANPAD that may be headed its way. The threat level for the A-10 in Iraq was much higher than in Afghanistan, but that is not to say that operations in the latter theatre were without risk of enemy fire – there were multiple recorded instances of accurate AAA against Hogs down low. *(USAF)*

ABOVE A crew chief marshals in an A-10C for munitions disarming after an October mission at Al Asad Air Base, Iraq, in 2007. The newly arrived C models – debuting in combat – were assigned to the 104th Expeditionary Fighter Squadron, a rainbow unit made up primarily of members from the 175th FW, Maryland Air National Guard. *(USAF)*

operations forces (SOF) team, but heavy pockets of Taliban and concentrations of organised resistance were seldom encountered. Meanwhile, A-10 units continued to rotate in and out of Bagram as part of the AEF cycle.

As 2002 gave way to 2003 America's gaze

BELOW A pilot assigned to the 104th Expeditionary Fighter Squadron prepares an A-10C for a mission in May 2012, at Bagram Airfield, Afghanistan. The tradition of painting either a hog or a shark mouth on the nose of the A-10 is religiously followed by many A-10 units. *(USAF)*

shifted once more to Iraq, and on 19 March that year, the 'shock and awe' campaign that was Operation Iraqi Freedom was unleashed. For the A-10, a renewed all-out shooting war in Iraq meant more CAS, CSAR and AFAC, to include working with the US Army's AH-64 Apache helicopters.

In October came a sea change in capability in the form of the AAQ-28 Litening target pod. Carried under the right wing, this pod replaced the 'poor man's FLIR' Maverick as a way of finding, identifying and then engaging enemies by night. The 354th FS deployed from Davis-Monthan to both Bagram, Afghanistan, and Kirkuk, Iraq, becoming the first Active Duty unit to use the pod in combat. The pod featured a laser designator and a laser spot tracker – the latter offering the same fundamental functionality as the ubiquitous Pave Penny – that allowed it to designate targets for its own laser-guided bombs, or for laser-guided weapons fired from other platforms.

For autonomous attacks using the pod, the GBU-12 500lb LGB was the weapon of choice. It featured Paveway guidance and fin kits strapped to the casing of a standard Mk 82 Low-Drag General Purpose bomb. In the nose of the guidance kits was a seeker head that pivoted in the relative airflow, identified the coded laser pulse coming from the Litening pod and issued control deflection commands to the nose-mounted guidance fins to steer the bomb to target. The GBU-12 was, and remains, an exceptionally effective weapon.

Combat operations in both Iraq and Afghanistan ebbed and flowed throughout the 2000s, with particular effort expended on ousting the Taliban from its footholds in the east of the landlocked country. Enduring Freedom was 'quiet' between April 2002 and late 2005, but things picked up in spring and summer 2006 as a rested Taliban fought with new energy in the south of the country, and the 303rd FS and 81st FS found themselves regularly supporting SOF and standard infantry units of the multinational International Security Assistance Force (ISAF) in southern Afghanistan.

Where Joint Terminal Attack Controllers on the ground were equipped with a ROVER handheld terminal, the A-10s were able to share video from their Litening pods both to

deliver better deconfliction with friendly forces on the ground and to enjoy greater efficacy in killing the enemy. While airburst weapons and GBU-12s provided excellent effects against targets away from civilian or friendly forces, the A-10s CAS work had increasingly fallen into the 'danger close' category, meaning that the pilot was employing ordnance within 50m of friendly positions. In these instances the gun was the weapon of choice, and it was noteworthy that in 2007 a pilot might shoot in excess of 11,000 rounds in one AEF rotation – an entire expeditionary squadron would have expended about that much in a typical 2003 AEF rotation.

In October 2007 the A-10Cs of the 104th EFS (a rainbow squadron of the 104th FS, Maryland ANG, and the 172nd FS, Michigan ANG) arrived in Afghanistan. They had originally been deployed to Iraq, making the type's combat debut and dropping the first GBU-38 Joint Direct Attack Munition 500lb GPS-guided bomb in the process, but a shortage of A-10s and the closure of A-10 squadrons as part of the Base Realignment and Closure programme meant that there were not enough to deploy to both theatres. The CAS mission in Afghanistan was given priority, and so the Hogs were moved.

Political progress, if it can be called that, was continuing to build in Afghanistan through late 2007. The Afghan National Army (ANA) had been formed, and in Kabul a government of sorts had been established. The ISAF now started to work towards getting the ANA to lead

combat operations. While in practice it was still ISAF teams that ran the show, for the A-10s it made little difference; they were still supporting troops on the ground.

The A-10C was making the execution of that mission much easier. It was also allowing the Hog squadrons to be more aggressive in the missions they took. With a space-stabilised target designation system like the Litening pod, a C-model pilot could designate a point of interest in the pod video feed (or the HUD), then create a set of GPS coordinates from it. This meant he could fly away from the point of interest, plan an attack, then come back and engage knowing that he would be able to find the target (or targets) again. Likewise, the C model's new moving map allowed low-level operations in mountainous terrain (flying into valleys) when the visibility was poor. The A-10C's stepbrother, the ANG and AFRes A-10A+, saw combat for the first time in Iraq in summer 2007 and debuted in Afghanistan in May 2008.

In July 2009 AFG A-10 operations moved from Bagram to Kandahar, the latter providing a better base from which to support the growing ISAF presence in the south of the country. By 2010, CAS combat operations in the Helmand province were so intense that A-10s were employing more 30mm rounds in weight than any other in-theatre squadron was employing in bombs and rockets.

In June 2011 the United States announced its intention to withdraw its forces from

ABOVE With the beauty of the mountains in the background, the juxtaposition between grizzled A-10s on the Bagram ramp and picture-postcard landscape must have been strange. When the A-10s first arrived at the former Soviet airfield, conditions were austere indeed. *(USAF)*

TOP AND ABOVE Bagram offered the A-10 the full range of environmental challenges, from snow and rain in the winter to barren heat in the summer. These shark-mouth A-10As carry a mix of rockets, Mk 82s and a single Maverick. *(USAF)*

Afghanistan, leaving behind only a small advisory force. The Hogs relocated back to Bagram in 2011 and thereafter continued to support the ANA and the shrinking contingent of Coalition advisers, infantry and special forces teams on the ground.

In 2013 the Scorpion helmet-mounted integrated targeting (HMIT) modification entered operational service. Scorpion gives the A-10C pilot the ability to spend much more time heads-up, looking outside. It projects colour symbology on to a monocle in front of the right eye, displaying key flight, weapons and navigation information: where the target pod is looking, where the rest of the flight is located, where the current steer point is and so on.

In February 2014 the Air Force announced its intention (once again!) to retire the A-10 and save $3.5 billion in operating costs over five years. The reality was somewhat different, and with the rise of the terrorist group Islamic State in Iraq and Syria, the A-10 was needed more than ever.

In December 2014 Operation Enduring Freedom finally came to an end with the handover of security operations to the Afghan government. That wasn't the end of the A-10's Afghan adventures, however. In late 2016 Hog squadrons continue to deploy to protect US, Coalition and Afghan forces.

Libya – Operation Odyssey Dawn

Six A-10s took part in Operation Odyssey Dawn (OOD) in March 2011. OOD was the US name for the UN-approved operation to enforce Security Council Resolution 1973, which later became known by the NATO codename Operation Unified Protector.

Combat operations over Libya posed a political challenge to the United States because

LEFT An A-10C of the 355th Fighter Wing, Davis-Monthan Air Force Base, Arizona, takes fuel from a KC-135 in mid-2010. Noteworthy is the presence of the AAQ-33 Sniper SE pod on the left wing. Sniper provides better range and capabilities than the AAQ-28 Litening pod, including two-video sharing and better IR video. *(USAF)*

Two A-10Cs from Spangdahlem's 81st FS prepare to take on fuel. The squadron, which had committed its A-10s to combat over the Balkans in the 1990s, was once again in the thick of it over Libya during Operation Odyssey Dawn in 2011. *(USAF)*

the official mandate of the Coalition was to enforce a no-fly zone, not provide support to Libyan rebel organisations on the ground attempting to overthrow the country's ruler, Muammar Gaddafi.

In reality, A-10s from the 81st FS deployed from Spangdahlem AB, Germany, to Aviano AB, Italy, and worked with CIA and British SAS troops on the ground to provide CAS to rebel forces. They also worked autonomously, engaging targets of opportunity. While generally very tight-lipped about who was doing what, Pentagon Press briefings were more forthcoming about employing A-10Cs to protect civilian populations that were 'under threat' by regime forces.

Of the few confirmed combat actions conducted by A-10s in Libya is the 28 March engagement of two small Libyan Coast Guard vessels, strafed with the GAU-8/A after they fired indiscriminately at merchant vessels in the port of Misrata.

Syria – Operation Inherent Resolve

When combat operations began against Islamic State targets in August 2014, Hogs of the 163rd EFS deployed to Al Jaber, Kuwait, and operated under the 332nd AEG.

Official statistics from 2015 show that at that time A-10s had flown around 11% of Operation Inherent Resolve sorties – striking IS targets in Iraq and Syria – compared to 41% by F-16s and 37% by F-15Es. However, the first A-10 OIR combat sorties were flown only in November, so that figure should be taken in context.

OIR rotations last 180 days, and the A-10 is providing support to Special Forces units on the ground, while also engaging in interdiction of IS targets. In one famous engagement in November 2015, A-10s worked with AC-130 Gunships to destroy a convoy of 116 tanker trucks near Abul Kamal, Syria.

ABOVE The Idaho ANG's 163rd EFS was the first A-10 unit to engage Islamic State forces when it deployed to Kuwait for an AEF rotation in 2014. *(USAF)*

BELOW Returning from a combat deployment is a cause for celebration. Here, fire trucks salute returning members of the Idaho Air National Guard. *(USAF)*

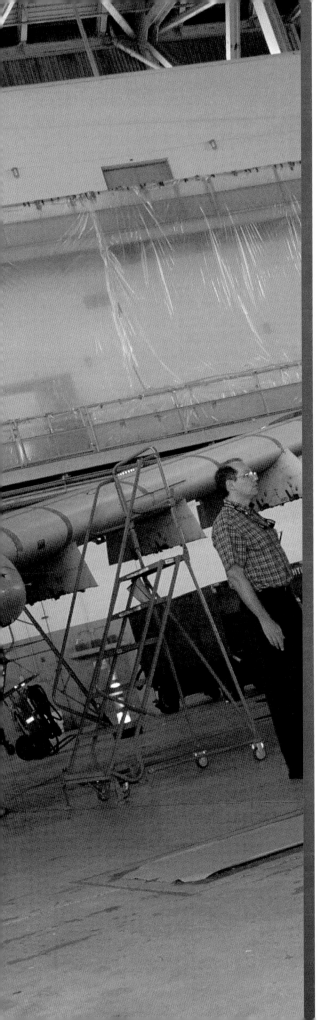

Chapter Five

Anatomy of the A-10C

Built from the outset with simplicity in mind, the A-10 lacks the sophistication of contemporaneous fighters like the F-16, F-15 and F/A-18. But 'simple' is usually anything but simple to deliver, and the A-10 is a marvel of engineering design and construction. Rugged, robust, redundant, the anatomy of the A-10 is the key to its ability to absorb punishment, operate in austere environments, and keep flying even when the ops tempo reaches fever pitch.

OPPOSITE On loan from the Maryland Air National Guard, this A-10C is undergoing computerised diagnostic measurement at Eglin Air Force Base, Florida. Using V-STAR, or Virtual Surveillance Target Attack Radar System technology, the system generates a three-dimensional image of the aircraft to help engineers out-fit the A-10 for smart weapons. *(USAF)*

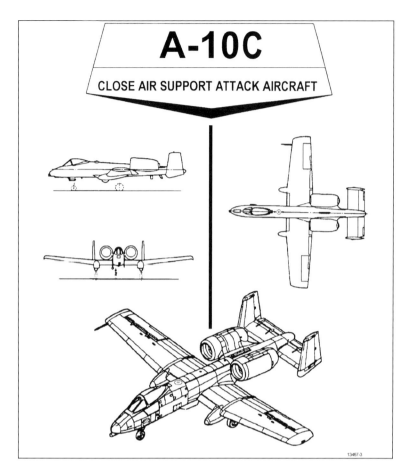

A-10C

CLOSE AIR SUPPORT ATTACK AIRCRAFT

13467-3

The A-10C is a single-seat close air support aircraft manufactured by the Fairchild Republic Company, Farmingdale, New York. It has a low-wing, low-tail configuration with two high bypass turbofan engines installed in nacelles mounted on pylons extending from the aft fuselage. Twin vertical stabilisers are mounted on the outboard tips of the horizontal tail.

The tricycle forward retracting landing gear is equipped with an anti-skid system and a steerable nose-wheel. The nose gear is installed to the right of the aircraft centreline to permit near-centreline gunfire. The nose gear retracts fully into the fuselage while the main gears partially retract into streamlined pods in the wings.

A titanium armour installation surrounds the cockpit, and the elevator and aileron controls split into redundant separate systems before leaving the protection of this armoured

RIGHT The Hog's general layout is dominated by the podded engines at rear, fuel tanks in the central fuselage and wings and massive GAU-8/A in the nose. Noteworthy is the auxiliary power unit nestled between the engines, which gives the A-10 pilot the ability to start his engines without relying on external equipment. *(USAF)*

FIRE EXTINGUISHER BOTTLES
RUDDER
AILERON/SPEED BRAKE
CONTROL TAB
TF-34-GE-100 ENGINE
TRIM TAB
ELEVATOR
PITOT-STATIC BOOM
LEFT MAIN TANK (AFT)
RIGHT MAIN TANK (FORWARD)
FLAPS
RIGHT WING TANK
COCKPIT ARMOR PLATE ASSEMBLY
RIGHT SYSTEM HYDRAULIC RESERVOIR
AUXILIARY POWER UNIT
ENVIR. CONTROL UNIT
LEFT SYSTEM HYDRAULIC RESERVOIR
AIR REFUEL RECEPTACLE (ARRS)
SLAT
ELECTRICAL EQUIP. AREA
SINGLE-POINT REFUELING
LEFT WING TANK
AMMO DRUM
GAU-8A GUN
13467-4

ABOVE An A-10C of the Arkansas Air National Guard's 188th Fighter Wing returns home from a deployment to Bagram Airfield, Afghanistan, in 2012. The centreline tank has a 600-gallon capacity. *(USAF)*

'bathtub'. The primary flight controls are equipped with artificial feel devices to simulate aerodynamic feel, but are powered by two independent hydraulic systems, either of which has the capability of controlling the aeroplane. If both hydraulic systems fail, the aeroplane can be flown using a manual reversion system.

The ailerons are of a clamshell design, consisting of upper and lower panels that split open to become speed brakes. The windshield front panel is resistant to small arms fire and birds. The windshield side panels are resistant to spall spray caused by penetrations.

The fuselage fuel cell sumps are self-sealing on the lower portion and tear-resistant on the upper portion. The cells are filled with a flexible foam to prevent fuel tank explosion. Single-point ground refuelling and engine feed lines are self-sealing.

The escape system provides a zero/zero capability (zero velocity and zero pitch and roll attitude) either with the canopy removed or through the canopy.

The armament system includes a high fire rate 30mm seven-barrel gun with ammunition stored in a drum. A variety of stores are carried on 11 pylons, four on each wing and three on the fuselage.

The overall dimensions of the aircraft under normal conditions of gross weight, tyre and strut inflation are as follows:

- Overall length 53ft 4in.
- Wingspan 57ft 6in.
- Horizontal tail span 18ft 10in.
- Height to top of fin 14ft 8in.
- Wheel base 17ft 9in.
- Wheel tread 17ft 3in.

The aircraft operating weight is approximately 28,000lb. This includes pilot, gun (full of ammunition), 11 empty pylons, oil, windshield wash and unusable fuel.

Fairchild Republic A-10 Thunderbolt II. *(Mike Badrocke)*

1 Cannon muzzle
2 Nose fairing
3 ILS antenna
4 Radar warning receiver (RWR) antennas
5 Air refuelling receptacle, open
6 Nosewheel bay offset to starboard
7 Cannon barrels
8 Rotary cannon bearing
9 Gun bay venting air intake
10 L-band antenna
11 Electrical equipment bay
12 Windscreen rain dispersal air duct
13 AAS-35 Pave Penny laser marked target receiver pod
14 Armoured windscreen
15 Head-up Display (HUD) symbol generator
16 HUD screen
17 Stand-by compass
18 Instrument panel shroud
19 Air refuelling feed pipe
20 Titanium armour 'bathtub' cockpit enclosure
21 Rudder pedals
22 Battery
23 General Electric GAU-8/A 30mm seven-barrelled rotary cannon
24 Ammunition feed and cartridge case return chutes
25 Nosewheel steering unit
26 Nose undercarriage leg strut
27 Forward retracting nosewheel
28 Torque scissor links
29 Retractable boarding ladder
30 Ventilating air outlets
31 Ladder stowage box
32 Pilot's side console panel
33 Engine throttle levers
34 Control column
35 McDonnell Douglas ACES II ejection seat
36 Headrest and canopy breakers
37 Upward hinging cockpit canopy
38 Canopy hinge link
39 Growth space for additional avionics equipment
40 Incidence transmitter
41 Electro-luminescent formation lighting strip
42 Canopy emergency release
43 Ventral gun bay access panels
44 Ammunition drum, 1,174 rounds
45 Ammunition bay armoured lining
46 Electrical system servicing panel and circuit breakers
47 Wing root fuselage strake
48 Cartridge case return chute
49 Control cable runs
50 Avionics equipment bays, port and starboard
51 Forward/centre fuselage production break
52 Antenna selector switches
53 IFF antenna
54 UHF/TACAN antenna
55 Anti-collision light
56 Starboard wing integral fuel tank
57 Over-wing tank filler
58 Machined wing skin/stringer panelling
59 Outer wing panel attachment bolted joint strip
60 Starboard wing weapons pylons, all pylons permanently fixed
61 CBU-87 sub-munition dispenser
62 AN/ALQ-131 ECM pod

63 Dedicated ECM pod pylon
64 Pitot head
65 Starboard down-turned wing-tip fairing
66 Wing tip mounted ALE-40 chaff/flare launchers (x 4)
67 Starboard navigation (green) and strobe (white) lights
68 Split aileron/deceleron mass balance
69 Deceleron open position
70 Starboard aileron/deceleron
71 Deceleron hydraulic jack
72 Aileron hydraulic actuator
73 Control linkages
74 Aileron tab
75 Tab mass balance weight
76 Single-slotted two-segment trailing edge flaps
77 Outboard flap hydraulic jack
78 Flap synchronising shafts, gear driven
79 Fuselage self-sealing fuel cell, max internal fuel capacity 6,066 litres (1,334 Imp gal)
80 Fuselage main longeron
81 Longitudinal control cable and services duct
82 Conditioned air delivery duct
83 Wing attachment fuselage main frames
84 Fuselage tank gravity fillers
85 Engine pylon fairing
86 Pylon main frame attachment joint
87 Starboard intake
88 Intake conical fairing
89 Fan blades
90 Machined engine mounting frames
91 Nacelle frame structure
92 Engine oil tank
93 General Electric TF-34-GE-100 turbofan engine
94 Rear engine mounting strut
95 Pylon trailing edge fillet fairing
96 Core engine (hot stream) exhaust duct
97 Fan air (cold stream) exhaust duct
98 Rudder hydraulic actuator
99 Starboard fin
100 X-Band antenna
101 Rudder mass balance weight
102 Starboard rudder
103 Elevator tab
104 Tab control rod
105 Starboard elevator

106 Starboard tailplane
107 Tailplane attachment frames
108 Elevator tandem hydraulic actuators
109 Tailcone
110 Tail navigation light
111 Rear RWR receiving antennas
112 ECM antenna
113 Honeycomb elevator structure
114 Port fin structure
115 Formation lighting strip
116 Honeycomb rudder panel
117 Port rudder hydraulic actuator
118 Rear identification light
119 Navigational antennas
120 Fin ventral fairing, stressed as tail bumper
121 Tailplane three-spar and rib torsion box structure
122 Tail control links
123 Port engine exhaust duct
124 Tailboom frame structure
125 VHF/AM antenna
126 Fuel jettison outlet
127 VHF/FM antenna
128 Fuel jettison duct
129 Hydraulic reservoir
130 Port engine nacelle attachment fitting
131 Cooling system intake/exhaust duct
132 Engine bleed air ducting
133 Auxiliary Power Unit (APU)
134 APU exhaust
135 Hinged engine nacelle access door
136 Environmental control system equipment pack
137 Port engine intake
138 Trailing edge wing root fillet

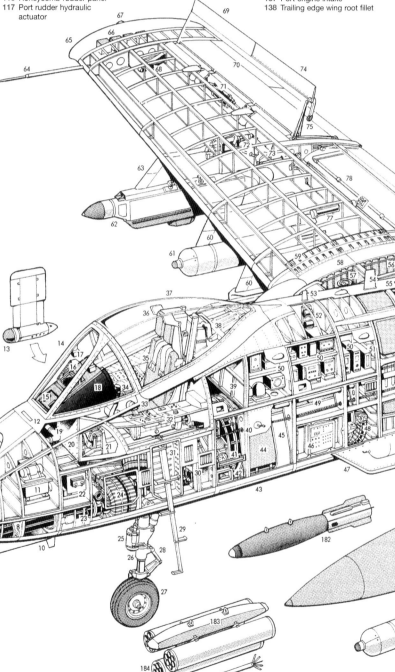

139 Port inboard single-slotted
flap segment
140 Flap guide rails
141 Undercarriage sponson
fairing mounted ALE-
40, 25-round chaff-flare
launchers (x 4)
142 Rear spar
143 Flap shroud structure
144 Honeycomb trailing edge
panel
145 Outboard flap segment
146 Port deceleron, open
position
147 Aileron tab
148 Aileron hinges

149 Port split aileron/deceleron
150 Down-turned wing tip
fairing frame structure
151 Port navigation (red) and
strobe (white) lights
152 Wing-tip formation lighting
strips
153 Port wing-tip ALE-40 chaff/
flare launchers (x 4)

154 Leading edge honeycomb
panels
155 Wing rib structure
156 Centre spar
157 Leading edge spar
158 Outboard pylons, 454kg
(1,000lb) capacity each

159 Twin missile carrier and
launch rails
160 AIM-9L Sidewinder self-
defence air-to-air missiles
161 CBU-87 sub-munition
dispenser
162 AGM-65A Maverick air-to-
surface missile
163 CBU-87 sub-munition
dispenser
164 Maverick launch rail
165 Port mainwheel
166 1,134kg (2,500lb) capacity
wing pylon
167 Main undercarriage leg strut
168 Mainwheel leg doors
169 Leg pivot mounting
170 Outer wing panel multi-bolt
attachment joint
171 Mainwheel semi-recessed
housing, protects airframe
in the event of a wheels-up
landing
172 Pressure refuelling
connection

173 Port mainwheel fairing
174 Wing root slat endplate
175 Port wing integral fuel tank
176 Inner wing panel rib
structure
177 Inboard leading edge slat
178 Slat hydraulic jacks
179 1,588kg (3,500lb) capacity
fuselage pylon (x 3)
180 Fuselage weapons stations
(x 3), two outboard or one
centreline only used at any
one time
181 2,271 litre (500 Imp gal)
external fuel tank
182 Mk 82 AIR 227kg (500lb)
retarded bomb
183 Triple ejector rack
184 LAU-68 7-round target
marking rocket pod (OA-10)
185 2¾in FFAR (Folding Fin
Aerial Rocket)

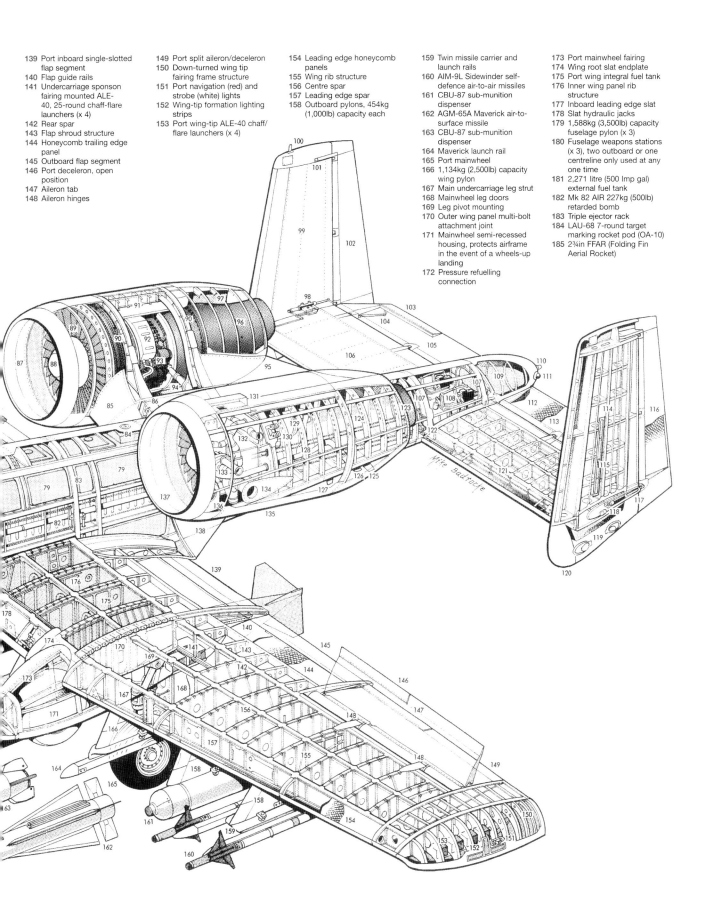

RIGHT The A-10 fuel system, like many of the Hog's other systems, is designed to be redundant and simple. Note the cut-offs that actuate when the pilot pulls any of the dash-mounted APU or engine fire handles. *(USAF)*

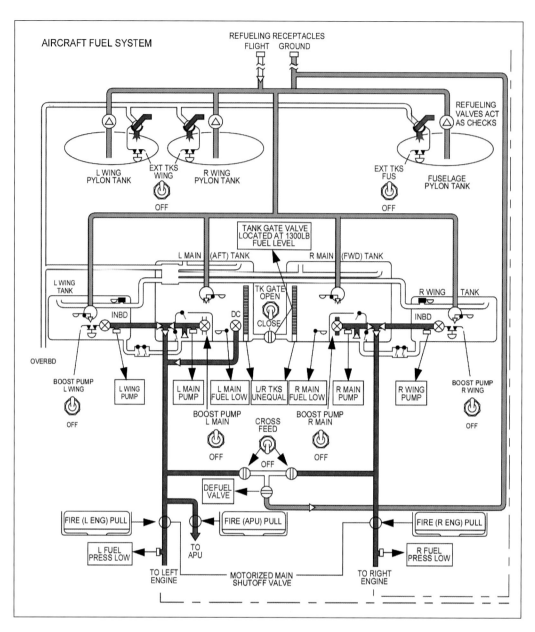

Aircraft fuel system

The aircraft fuel supply system consists of two internal wing tanks (left and right wings) and two tandem-mounted fuselage tanks (left main-aft and right main-forward). Up to three external (pylon) tanks may also be carried, one tank on each wing and one on the fuselage centreline.

The fuel supply system operates as two independent subsystems, with the left wing and left main tank feeding the left engine and the APU (auxiliary power unit), and the right wing and right main tank feeding the right engine. The two subsystems can be interconnected by opening cross-feed valves (controlled by a single switch in the cockpit) to allow pressurised fuel flow to both engines and the APU from either subsystem.

In addition, the two main tanks can be interconnected by opening a tank gate valve (also a single cockpit switch). The main tank sumps are self-sealing bladder cells. Each self-sealing sump contains approximately 900lb of fuel. The upper portions of the cells are tear-resistant bladders. The wing tanks are integral within the wing structure and do not have bladder cells. Foam is incorporated in each tank to prevent fuel tank explosion.

Boost pressure is provided by boost pumps located in each main and wing tank. A DC boost pump, located in the left main tank, is used during engine and APU starts if the left main boost pump is inoperative. For negative g flight, collector tanks will supply the engine with sufficient fuel for ten seconds' operation at maximum power.

The wing tank boost pumps operate at a higher pressure and override the main tank boost pumps to automatically empty the wing tanks first. The main fuel feed lines to each engine, and to the APU, contain shut-off valves that are controlled by the fire handles. These shut-off valves allow for isolation of the fuel feed system outside the tanks.

Fuel in the external tanks is transferred to the main or wing tanks by pressure from the bleed air system. Fuel tank sump drains are provided for each tank. Drain valves can be opened externally. Fuel cavity drains are provided in each main tank and protrude through the aircraft skin to give an indication of fuel cell leaks.

The wing tanks have a dual-level refuelling shut-off valve. The valve closes when the tank is full and will not reopen unless the fuel level drops approximately 400lb or a time delay of approximately ten minutes has elapsed.

Wing tanks cannot be topped off unless the fuel level is below approximately 1,590lb or the fuel manifold has been unpressurised for the time-delay period. This assures even fuel transfer from the external tanks. Therefore during fuel transfer from the external tanks the wing-tank fuel quantity will drop approximately 400lb, then will fill to capacity. This cycling repeats until external fuel is depleted. During air refuelling the wing tanks will not accept fuel unless the fuel level in the tanks has dropped approximately 400lb or the time delay has elapsed. The total fuel on board after refuelling could be approximately 800lb less than total capacity.

If total fuel capacity is required during air refuelling, the external tanks can be turned off sufficiently prior to refuelling so that the wing-tank quantity drops approximately 400lb or the time delay has elapsed.

A single-point ground-refuelling receptacle, located in the leading edge of the left landing gear nacelle, permits refuelling of each internal and external tank. A control panel adjacent

to the refuelling receptacle provides a means of ground-checking the refuelling valve shut-off. The panel also permits selective loading of any internal or external tank. Auxiliary DC essential bus power is required for refuelling valve checks, selective tank filling, and to enable external tank filling. When the tanks are full the refuelling valves are closed by a float valve in each tank.

When carrying external tanks, fuel sequencing is as follows:

■ External wing tanks.
■ External fuselage tank.
■ Internal fuel.

TOP AND ABOVE
Since 2010 the Air Force has evaluated a 50/50 blend of hydrotreated renewable jet and JP-8 – so called biomass-derived jet fuel blend – making the A-10 the first aircraft to be fuelled this way. Here a maintainer prepares to attach the refuelling hose to an A-10's single refuelling point in the port (left) wing pod. *(USAF)*

Air refuelling system

The aircraft can be refuelled in flight from a boom-equipped tanker. It is equipped with a UARRSI (Universal Aerial Refueling Receptacle Slipway Installation) located forward of the cockpit. By positioning a lever on the fuel system control panel, a flush (slipway) door, powered by the right hydraulic system, folds down into the fuselage to expose the air refuelling receptacle and to provide a slipway to guide the tanker boom. When the tanker boom is inserted in the receptacle, the nozzle latch rollers are actuated to the locked position and refuelling transfer commences. Fuel transfer through the receptacle is distributed to the main and wing tanks, and to external tanks if carried. Disable switches, located on the fuel system control panel, allow fuel to be prevented from entering any specific internal tank suspected of being damaged.

As each tank is filled, float-operated fuel shut-off valves within the tank will close, preventing overfill. When refuelling is complete, disconnection of the boom nozzle will normally be accomplished by a signal from the tanker or by the receiver depressing the air refuel disconnect/reset button – nose-wheel steering (NWS) button – on the control-stick grip. An automatic disconnect will occur when both receiver and tanker systems are completely operational and one of the following happens:

- Excessive fuel pressure occurs in the receiver fuel manifold.
- Tanker boom limits are exceeded.

If the right hydraulic system fails, the spring-loaded slipway door will open when the air refuel control is set to 'OPEN'. The time for the door to open sufficiently to expose the receptacle is improved by reducing speed and will occur within approximately three minutes at 150 KIAS (knots indicated airspeed). Aerodynamic effect will open the door sufficiently to expose the receptacle lights and permit emergency 'stiff boom' refuelling with or without a 'READY' light. Applying boom nozzle pressure on the slipway door should result in the slipway door downlock engaging and a 'READY' light. The 'LATCHED' and 'DISCONNECT' light will not come on in this case.

Electrical power system

The electrical power system provides DC and AC power. A battery produces DC to power essential equipment, which provides the aircraft with a limited instrument flight capability. The instrument inverter changes DC from the battery to AC to power essential equipment.

DC produced by the battery is adequate

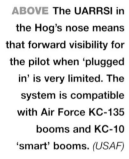

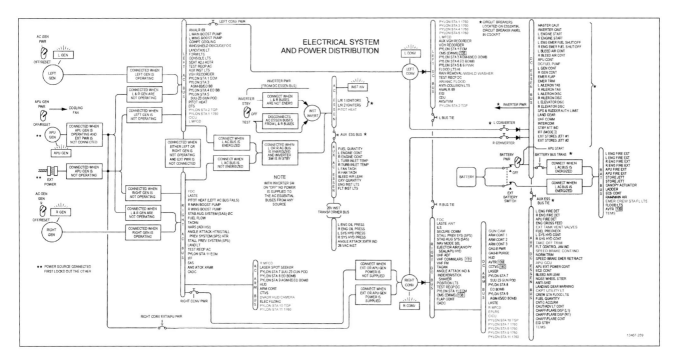

to start the APU. When operational, the APU generator produces sufficient AC and DC (through the converters) to power all electrical busses indefinitely, provided electrical load is minimised. With engines running, two generators take over production of AC and DC (through the converters) to power all busses. External power can also be used to power all AC and DC (through the converters) busses.

DC system

Battery
The battery is a 24V nickel cadmium type. It supplies DC to the battery, DC essential and auxiliary DC essential busses.

Battery bus
The battery bus provides DC so that certain equipment can be operated when the cockpit battery switch is off.

DC essential bus and auxiliary DC essential bus
The DC essential and auxiliary DC essential busses provide DC to equipment deemed crucial for flight.

Converter caution lights
The left and right converter caution lights come on to indicate failure of the associated converter.

ABOVE The electrical system and power distribution schematic shows how left and right generators feed AC power to their respective busses, and also feed to DC converters that in turn power left and right DC busses. *(USAF)*

BELOW The A-10C caution light panel is located by the pilot's right knee and has captions that illuminate when a given system fails or reaches a predefined level. A master caution light is located on the glare shield, and will flash to prompt the pilot to check his caution panel for an illuminated caption. *(USAF)*

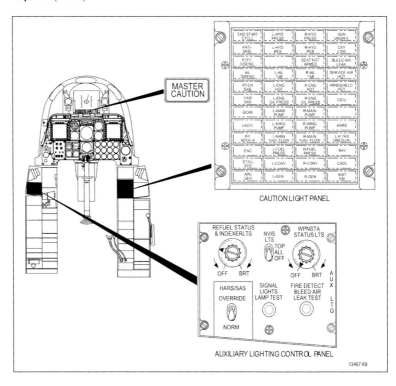

Left DC bus, right DC bus and DC armament bus

The left DC, right DC, and DC armament busses provide DC to mission support equipment and those systems not deemed essential to flight.

AC system

Instrument inverter

The instrument inverter changes DC supplied by the battery to AC. AC from the inverter powers the AC essential, auxiliary AC essential and AC instrument transformer busses, when the left and right AC busses are not energised.

AC essential bus, auxiliary AC essential bus and AC instrument transformer bus

The AC essential, auxiliary AC essential and instrument transformer busses power equipment needed for starting engines and operating engine instruments.

Integrated drive generators

An integrated drive generators unit is mounted on each engine. Each IDG consists of a drive system and an AC generator.

Generators

Left and right generators produce AC power.

Each is capable of supplying sufficient power for all AC busses, and either one will automatically pick up the load if the other fails. Cockpit control of the generators is provided by generator switches.

External power

External power can be used to supply all AC busses directly, and all DC busses through the converters. A standard receptacle, located on the forward underside of the fuselage, provides a ground connection for external power. Inserting the plug of the external power unit depresses a contactor button and enables the system.

When power is available from both the external source and APU generator, the first one selected automatically locks out the other. With external power supplied to the aircraft, the first engine-driven generator to come on line will supply power to its associated bus, and the external source will continue to supply the opposite system. When the second engine-driven generator comes on line the external power is automatically locked out.

During engine shutdown, when the generator drops off the line, the associated left/right busses will be supplied with power from the external source, if one is connected.

Hydraulic power supply system

The hydraulic power supply system consists of two fully independent hydraulic power systems, designated left hydraulic system and right hydraulic system. Both are pressurised by identical engine-driven pumps. A small accumulator in each system stabilises the pressure.

In addition to the two system hydraulic pumps, an APU hydraulic pump can be selected for ground use only to provide hydraulic power to either hydraulic system, but not both simultaneously. The selector valve is accessible through the APU access door on the bottom of the aft fuselage.

The left hydraulic system powers the following systems:

- Flight control – left rudder, left elevator, left and right ailerons, flaps.

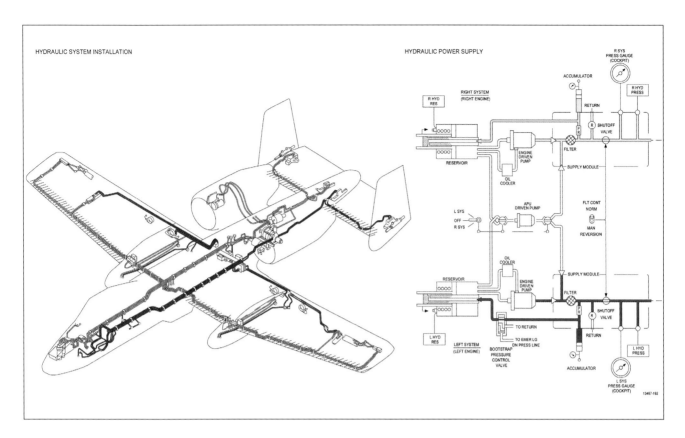

HYDRAULIC SYSTEM INSTALLATION

HYDRAULIC POWER SUPPLY

ABOVE Two hydraulic systems (left and right) power all of the A-10's flight controls. Note how the right-hand system powers the ailerons and the right elevator, and the left-hand system powers the flaps and the left elevator. *(USAF)*

BELOW Signalling that he's ready to fly and fight, a 422nd **TES** pilot steps on the rudder and steers an A-10C loaded with live ordnance out of the arming area at Nellis AFB, Nevada. The nose-wheel steering is powered by the left hydraulic system, as are the other landing-gear functions. *(Steve Davies/FJPhotography.com)*

- Landing gear – landing gear extend and retract, wheel brakes, anti-skid and NWS.
- Armament – half of gun drive.

The right hydraulic system powers the following systems:

- Flight control – right rudder, right elevator, left and right ailerons, speed brakes, slats.
- Emergency auxiliary landing gear systems extend, emergency wheel braking and associated accumulators.
- Armament – half of gun drive.
- Air refuelling – slipway door and receptacle lock.

The hydraulic systems are designed for combat survivability, and the left and right systems are physically separated as much as possible. The landing gear, gear uplock, wheel brake, and NWS lines are isolated from the left system pressure when the gear is up and locked. The landing gear and associated systems can also be isolated from the left hydraulic system by opening the 'LAND GEAR' circuit breaker. The speed brakes are isolated from right system pressure when the speed brake switch is in hold or by selecting 'SPD BK EMR RETR' on the emergency flight control panel. Flaps can be totally isolated from the left hydraulic system by selecting 'FLAP EMER RETR' on the emergency flight control panel.

Landing gear system

The landing gear system is a tricycle configuration with the main gear retracting into pods suspended below the wing and the nose gear retracting into the

BELOW While the A-10's main landing gear has a variety of redundant features built in to allow it to be extended even after loss of hydraulic pressure, the semi-retracted wheels design was deliberately chosen to give the pilot the option of a wheels-up landing if absolutely necessary. In fact the design works extremely well, and several A-10s have been saved as a result. *(USAF)*

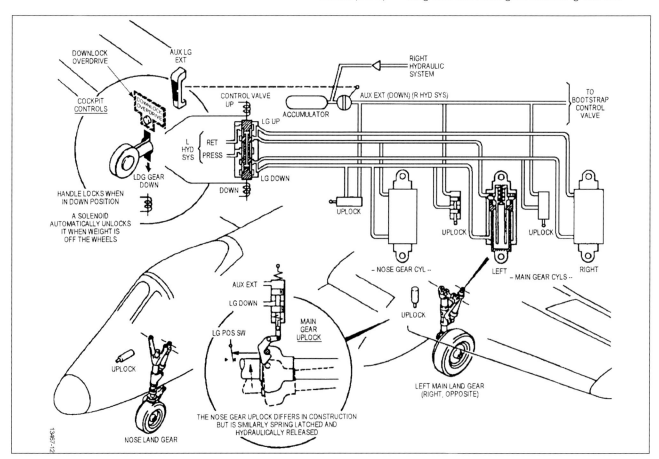

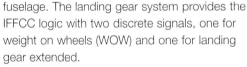

fuselage. The landing gear system provides the IFFCC logic with two discrete signals, one for weight on wheels (WOW) and one for landing gear extended.

The nose gear is offset to the right of the aircraft centreline to accommodate the centreline location of the 30mm gun. All three landing gear struts retract forward to aid free-fall auxiliary extension.

Landing gear extension and retraction is controlled by the landing gear handle and powered by the left hydraulic system. In the gear-retracted position, the system is depressurised and isolated. In the normal gear-down position, the system is pressurised.

Auxiliary extension of the landing gear is available in the event that left hydraulic system pressure is not present or if the landing gear handle or valve is jammed or failed. The system requires no electrical power.

The landing gear system includes a landing gear position and warning system, and a downlock override control. Switches sense gear and uplock position to provide cockpit indications and to depressurise/isolate the landing gear hydraulic system after retraction.

ABOVE LEFT AND ABOVE Designed to be operated from austere and rough forward operating locations, the A-10's main landing gear has thick shock struts to dampen out uneven terrain. Hog pilots regularly operate from the baked mud floor of the desert in Nevada, and forward operating locations in the desert were used by A-10s during Operation Desert Storm. *(Steve Davies/FJPhotography.com)*

Main landing gear (MLG)

The shock struts provide a rough field taxiing capability. The landing gear retracting cylinder is also the drag brace. A spring-powered mechanical downlock automatically engages both for powered and free-fall gear extensions, while switches provide cockpit indication of downlock.

For gear retraction, hydraulic pressure unlocks the downlock and then extends the retracting cylinder piston to push (rotate) the gear forward and up. As the gear approaches the upstop, an uplock is engaged. Gear up pressure automatically applies brake pressure to stop wheel rotation before the wheels retract into the gear pods. When retracted, a spring-loaded snubber contacts the tyre to prevent air-drag rotation of the wheels.

THIS PAGE The Hog's nose landing gear is positioned off-centre to the starboard (right) to allow the GAU-8/A barrel and supporting ammunition drive and feeds to fit. The gear features taxi and take-off/landing lights, although plans to add an IR light for covert operations have not been implemented. Even so, when the first A-10s operated from Bagram Airfield, Afghanistan, in 2002 they did so initially in complete darkness – no taxi or take-off lights and no external lighting. To do so, they relied entirely on their night vision goggles. *(Steve Davies/ FJPhotography.com)*

For gear extension, hydraulic pressure disengages the uplock hooks and simultaneously retracts the cylinder piston to pull down the gear. Extend pressure is maintained with the gear handle in 'DOWN'.

Nose landing gear (NLG)

The nose landing gear operates in a similar fashion to the main gear. As the strut extends when weight comes off the tyre, a cam centres the nose-wheel. Two doors seal off the fuselage compartment after gear retraction.

Nose-wheel steering system (NWS)

The NWS system is pressurised by the left hydraulic system. Damping is provided to prevent nose-wheel shimmy in the steering and swivel modes.

NWS is available only when the landing gear handle is 'DOWN' and weight is sensed on either main gear. Failure of the circuitry or loss of electrical power will revert the system to the swivel mode to prevent a hardover. A compensator on the steer/damp unit provides sufficient hydraulic fluid and pressure to retain the shimmy-damping function in the event of loss of hydraulic power.

The NWS button is located on the control-stick grip. With Low-Altitude Safety and Targeting Enhancement (LASTE) operating, and weight off the wheels, this button is used to command target pod laser firing. During air refuelling, it is used to disconnect from the refuelling tanker if the boom nozzle is inserted and the 'LATCHED' light is on, or to recycle the air refuelling system to the ready mode.

Wheel brake system

The normal wheel brake system is fully powered from the left hydraulic landing gear-down circuit. The brakes are independently activated by linkage from the rudder pedals.

For initial take-offs and normal landings, the brake system, in conjunction with fully extended speed brakes, is capable of stopping the aircraft throughout the range of acceptable gross weights and configurations.

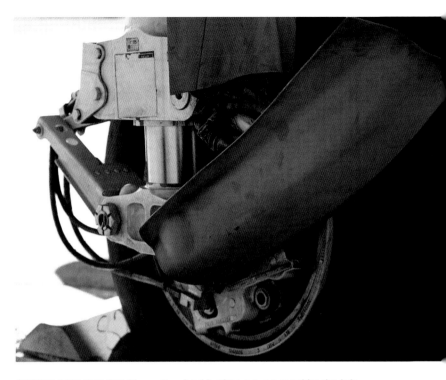

ABOVE AND BELOW The main wheel brakes are powered by the left hydraulic system, and feature an anti-skid mode that will cycle pressure on and off to stop the aircraft in the shortest distance without blowing a tyre. The system is particularly valuable in wet or damp weather. *(Steve Davies/FJPhotography.com)*

Emergency brake system

With the left hydraulic system failed and the right hydraulic system operative, the emergency brake system has the same capabilities as the normal system, minus anti-skid. In the event of a failure of both hydraulic systems, emergency braking power is provided by an accumulator serviced by, but isolated from, the right hydraulic system. In the event of loss of both hydraulic systems, sufficient accumulator fluid pressure is available for a minimum of five full-brake applications.

The system is activated by pulling the emergency brake handle and then actuating the brake pedals. Pulling the handle also actuates a switch that disables the anti-skid system.

The emergency braking system is fully independent of the normal system down to, but not including, the wheel brake cylinder.

Anti-skid control system

The anti-skid control system enables efficient maximum braking for all runway conditions. Cockpit controls and displays consist of an engage switch, an emergency disengage switch and a caution light.

During light and moderate braking the system usually does not operate. During heavy braking the anti-skid control system attempts to achieve a maximum deceleration rate. The system operates until it senses wheel rotation speed has decreased to 10kt.

Primary Flight Control System (PFCS)

Commands are transmitted via non-redundant pushrods from the stick to the aft area of the armoured cockpit (white area), through a set of control disconnectors, and then by redundant cables to the elevators and ailerons and by a single cable to the rudders.

Loss of one hydraulic system does not affect pitch and roll response, but does cause moderate increase in the pedal force required for yaw inputs. Jams in the pitch or roll control systems, aft of the disconnect units in the white area, may be isolated to free the stick for control of the unjammed portions.

Redundant control circuits provide for trim controls in the pitch and roll axis, while yaw trim is achieved through the yaw Stability Augmentation System (SAS). The dual channel SAS provides rate damping in both

RIGHT The A-10's flight controls hold one of the secrets to its ability to absorb punishment and still get the pilot either home or to a safe place for ejection. This schematic shows the old-fashioned 'rod and pulley' configuration of the Hog's flight controls. *(USAF)*

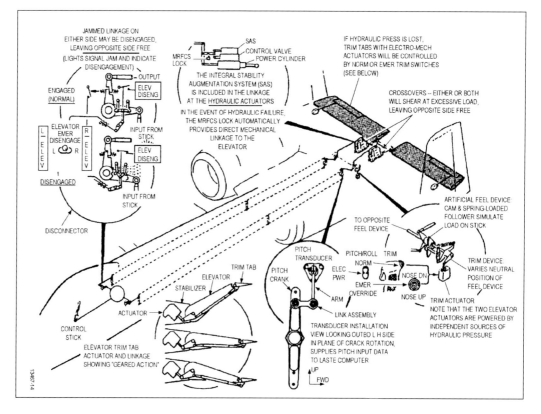

the pitch and yaw axes as well as automatic turn coordination.

Pitch control is provided by two elevators connected by a shearable crossover shaft. The elevators are powered by independent actuators, which are also connected by a shearable crossover shaft and powered by independent hydraulic systems. Inputs to the actuators are made via independent, widely separated cable and linkage paths that connect directly to the disconnector units. A single system of pushrods within the white area connects the disconnector units to the stick.

Because the elevators are connected, one actuator will power both elevators in the event of the loss of one hydraulic system. The actuators are connected so that both (and, in turn, both elevators) will be operated via a single mechanical control path in the event one control path is lost. Hence, loss of one hydraulic system and/or mechanical control path will have no discernible effect on stick/surface response.

If an elevator, elevator actuator or control path aft of the disconnector is jammed, the jammed side of the system can be disconnected using the elevator emergency disengage switch. Stick inputs will then shear the actuator crossover shaft and the elevator crossover shaft. This will free the unjammed side of the system.

If a jam occurs with appreciable elevator deflection, pitch authority in the opposite direction will be minimal – eg if an elevator is jammed with an upward deflection, pitch-down authority will be reduced.

Artificial stick feel is provided by devices located close to the elevator actuators and a bobweight located in the white area. Trim is provided by two independent electrical circuits: the normal pitch/roll trim control circuit and the emergency override pitch/roll trim circuit. These circuits lead to a trim motor that acts on the artificial feel device to reposition the actuators and move the entire elevator surface. If both hydraulic systems are lost, pitch trim inputs will automatically operate the two elevator trim tabs via two additional trim motors to provide pitch trim.

The geared/trimmable elevator tabs are mounted on the outboard trailing edges of both elevators. The tabs are trimmable in manual

reversion, and geared in the powered flight control mode. This reduces elevator aerodynamic loads to levels satisfactory for instantaneous transfer from powered mode to Manual Reversion Flight Control System (MRFCS).

Two identical and independent pitch SAS channels provide rate damping for enhanced tracking, and pitch trim compensation for speed brake deployment. A pitch transducer attached to a crank in the aft fuselage provides input data to the IFFCC for pitch attitude control (PAC).

Roll control system

The ailerons are powered by a tandem hydraulic actuator that normally allows each aileron to be powered by both hydraulic systems. Inputs to the actuators are made through independent, widely separated cable and linkage paths that connect through aileron tab shift mechanisms to the disconnect units. A single system of pushrods within the white area connects the disconnect units to the control stick.

TOP AND ABOVE

The A-10's elevators (shown here) and ailerons both feature trim tabs – small tabs that are electromechanically actuated to trim the aircraft for level flight. Crucially, the trim tabs operate when the pilot has entered the manual reversion mode, and in the case of the aileron trim tabs they offer the only way of directly controlling roll. (Steve Davies/ FJPhotography.com)

RIGHT An artificial feel device simulates control loads on the A-10's control stick. Even so, the aircraft still gives the pilot the sense that he's directly connected to the flight controls, even though the hydraulic systems, with inputs from the Stability Augmentation System (SAS), are driving the flight controls to the commanded position.
(USAF)

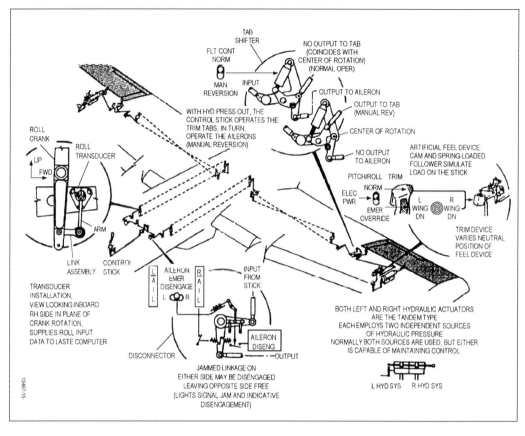

BELOW The A-10's ailerons are also clamshell-type speed brakes that split apart when actuated. When extended, the speed brakes continue to act as ailerons by rotating up and down in their open position, albeit with a more limited range of motion.
(Steve Davies/ FJPhotography.com)

If one hydraulic system is lost, the operative system will continue to power both ailerons. Hence the loss of one hydraulic system has no discernible effect on stick/surface response.

In the event one control path is lost, roll control will be provided by the connected aileron, and roll authority will be reduced by approximately one-half. Normal stick force relative to roll rate will be experienced, but the stick will have to be moved twice as much

for a given manoeuvre. If an aileron surface, aileron actuator or a control path aft of the disconnectors becomes jammed, the aileron emergency disengage switch can be used to free the unjammed aileron. If a jam occurs with appreciable aileron deflection, roll control in the opposite direction will be minimal – *eg* if right aileron is jammed with an upward deflection, roll authority to the left will be reduced.

Artificial stick feel is provided by redundant devices located close to the aileron actuators. Trim is provided by two independent electrical circuits: the normal pitch/roll trim control circuit and the emergency override pitch/roll trim circuit. These circuits lead to a trim motor in each wing. The trim motor acts on the artificial feel device, which in turn repositions the actuator to move the entire aileron surface. Sufficient trim for normal operations can be obtained from one trim motor. However, trim rate and authority will be reduced. Disengagement of an aileron will not cause loss of roll trim. No roll trim will be available in the manual reversion operating mode.

Aileron tabs are mounted on the inboard trailing edge of each aileron. During normal flight the tabs are geared to reduce aerodynamic

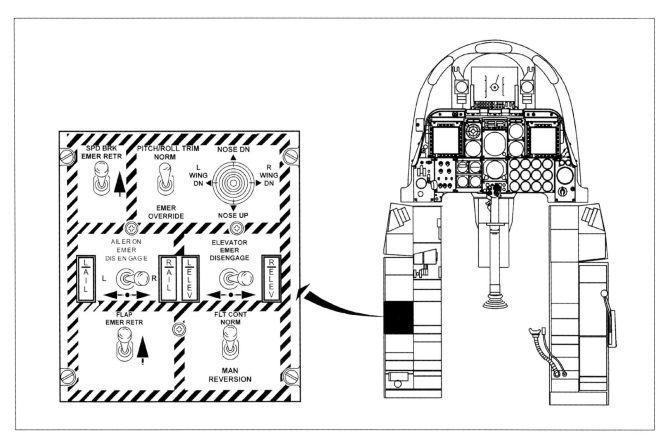

SPD BRK
EMER RETR

PITCH/ROLL TRIM
NORM

NOSE DN

L
WING
DN

R
WING
DN

EMER
OVERRIDE

NOSE UP

AIL ER ON
EMER
DIS EN GAG E

ELEVATOR
EMER
DISENGAGE

L
A
IL

L   R

R
A
IL

L
E
L
E
V

R
E
L
E
V

FLAP
EMER RETR

FLT CONT
NORM

MAN
REVERSION

loads on the ailerons, and are not directly controlled by lateral stick inputs. In manual reversion, lateral stick inputs are transmitted directly to the tabs, which in turn fly the ailerons.

A roll transducer attached to a crank in the forward fuselage provides input data to the IFFCC for PAC.

Emergency disengagement

Two three-position lever-locked switches, labelled 'ELEVATOR EMER DISENGAGE' and 'AILERON EMER DISENGAGE', are mounted on the emergency flight control panel. The disengage circuits are powered by the DC essential bus.

The switches are normally centred. In the event of the jamming of a control path aft of the disconnector units, or a jam in the actuator or control surface, a light adjacent to the appropriate switch will come on as abnormal stick force countering the jam is exerted. The stick is disconnected from the jammed side by moving the appropriate switch toward the light.

The stick becomes immediately free to control the unjammed control path. After disconnecting a jammed elevator, stick force will be momentarily higher than normal until the controllable elevator is displaced approximately 3° relative to the jammed surface, at which point the crossover shaft between the two elevator actuators will shear. The subsequent shearing of the elevator crossover shaft will be accomplished with hydraulic powered inputs.

For both elevator and aileron control jams, normal stick force per g relative to roll or pitch input is experienced, but the stick has to be moved or trimmed approximately twice as much for a given manoeuvre.

When a control path is not fully engaged at the disconnect unit, the 'ELEV DISENG' or 'AIL DISENG' light on the caution light panel comes on. When the switch is subsequently moved to the centre position or to disengage the opposite side, the surface will reconnect as soon as the stick is moved in alignment with the surface position.

Though remotely possible, both elevators or ailerons can be disconnected, but one surface will automatically reconnect as soon as the stick is moved into alignment with the position of the control surface.

ABOVE Emergency disconnection of the flight control surfaces from the hydraulics systems can occur automatically or when the pilot commands the system into the manual mode using this control panel. *(USAF)*

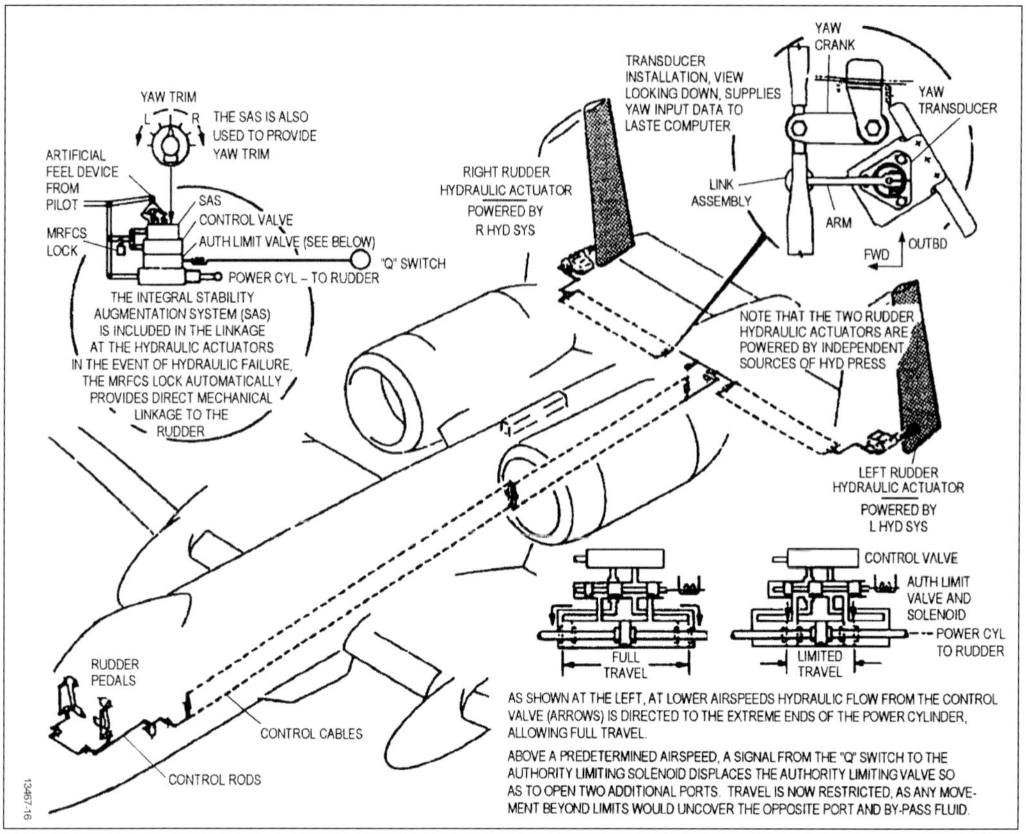

RIGHT Independent hydraulic actuators drive each of the A-10's two rudders, although these control surfaces do not have shearable links like the ailerons and elevators, and cannot be trimmed if MRFCS mode is entered. *(USAF)*

YAW TRIM
L R
THE SAS IS ALSO USED TO PROVIDE YAW TRIM

YAW CRANK

YAW TRANSDUCER

TRANSDUCER INSTALLATION, VIEW LOOKING DOWN, SUPPLIES YAW INPUT DATA TO LASTE COMPUTER

ARTIFICIAL FEEL DEVICE FROM PILOT

SAS
CONTROL VALVE
AUTH LIMIT VALVE (SEE BELOW)

MRFCS LOCK

POWER CYL – TO RUDDER

"Q" SWITCH

RIGHT RUDDER HYDRAULIC ACTUATOR POWERED BY R HYD SYS

LINK ASSEMBLY

ARM

FWD

OUTBD

THE INTEGRAL STABILITY AUGMENTATION SYSTEM (SAS) IS INCLUDED IN THE LINKAGE AT THE HYDRAULIC ACTUATORS IN THE EVENT OF HYDRAULIC FAILURE, THE MRFCS LOCK AUTOMATICALLY PROVIDES DIRECT MECHANICAL LINKAGE TO THE RUDDER

NOTE THAT THE TWO RUDDER HYDRAULIC ACTUATORS ARE POWERED BY INDEPENDENT SOURCES OF HYD PRESS

LEFT RUDDER HYDRAULIC ACTUATOR POWERED BY L HYD SYS

CONTROL VALVE
AUTH LIMIT VALVE AND SOLENOID
POWER CYL TO RUDDER

FULL TRAVEL

LIMITED TRAVEL

RUDDER PEDALS

CONTROL CABLES

CONTROL RODS

13467-16

AS SHOWN AT THE LEFT, AT LOWER AIRSPEEDS HYDRAULIC FLOW FROM THE CONTROL VALVE (ARROWS) IS DIRECTED TO THE EXTREME ENDS OF THE POWER CYLINDER, ALLOWING FULL TRAVEL.

ABOVE A PREDETERMINED AIRSPEED, A SIGNAL FROM THE "Q" SWITCH TO THE AUTHORITY LIMITING SOLENOID DISPLACES THE AUTHORITY LIMITING VALVE SO AS TO OPEN TWO ADDITIONAL PORTS. TRAVEL IS NOW RESTRICTED, AS ANY MOVEMENT BEYOND LIMITS WOULD UNCOVER THE OPPOSITE PORT AND BY-PASS FLUID.

Yaw control system

Yaw control is provided by two rudders, each of which is individually driven by independent hydraulic actuators. The actuators are controlled in unison by a single cable and linkage transmission path that connects to the rudder pedals.

RIGHT The A-10's vertical stabilisers provide excellent yaw stabilisation, which is particularly important when firing the Avenger, and have the added role of shielding the exhaust efflux from the side. The OT codes on this tail identify it as belonging to the 422nd TES, Nellis AFB, Nevada. *(Steve Davies/FJPhotography.com)*

Because there is a single control path, there is no disconnect capability in the event of a jam. However, if an actuator or rudder surface becomes jammed, some yaw control from the unjammed rudder may be available due to stretching of the connecting cables between the actuators. Required rudder pedal force will be significantly higher. Full trim authority will be available for the unjammed rudder if the yaw SAS channel on the jammed side is turned off.

If one hydraulic system is lost, slightly degraded rudder authority will result. Initial rudder pedal inputs will move only the powered rudder. Then, increases in rudder pedal input will move both the powered and unpowered rudders and the unpowered rudder will trail the powered rudder. Hence, the rudder pedals have to be moved more than normal and there will be a moderate increase in the pedal force required.

If both hydraulic power sources are lost, the actuators automatically shift modes to permit direct transfer of rudder pedal inputs to the rudder surfaces. Pedal forces in this mode are higher. Artificial rudder pedal feel and centring characteristics are integrated into both rudder actuators.

At aircraft speeds above 240 KIAS, available powered rudder travel is automatically reduced from ±25° to ±8°. If aircraft speed increases through approximately 240 KIAS with rudder inputs greater than ±8°, rudder pedal 'kicks' or 'thumps' may be felt as the rudder returns to 8°.

Independent SAS signals are electrically transmitted to each rudder actuator to provide automatic turn coordination, yaw damping and yaw trim. A yaw transducer attached to a crank in the aft fuselage provides input data to the IFFCC for PAC.

Pitch and roll trim control systems

The pitch and roll trim control systems are similar in function. Both act on the artificial feel devices to vary the zero load position of the stick and equivalent surface positions. A five-position switch, mounted at the top of the stick grip, is used for normal pitch/roll trim control.

Trim change is proportional to the time the button is activated. Trim rates are essentially independent of stick loading conditions. In the event of a failure in either the pitch or roll trim circuit, control of both trim axes may be transferred to an identical five-position switch located on the emergency flight control panel. The emergency pitch/roll trim circuitry is powered separately from the normal trim, although both circuits operate the same trim motors.

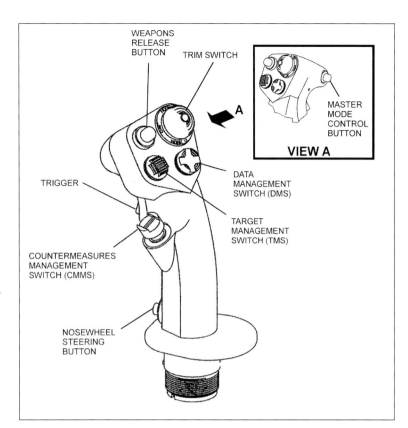

Take-off trim control system

When the 'T/O TRIM' button is depressed, the pitch and roll trim motors and the two elevator tab trim motors are driven to neutral. With the button depressed and the yaw trim knob and five trim motors at neutral setting, the 'TAKEOFF TRIM' light comes on.

ABOVE Pitch and roll trim is accessed via a traditional trim switch on the control stick. Pictured here is the A-10C stick, taken straight out of the F-16 and giving the pilot full HOTAS functionality. *(USAF)*

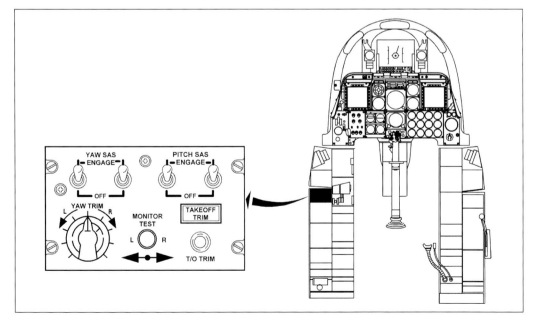

LEFT Depressing the take-off trim button drives the pitch and roll tabs to their neutral positions. *(USAF)*

Stability Augmentation System

The Stability Augmentation System enhances flying qualities for target tracking, reduces workload and provides yaw trim capability. Hydraulic power is required for the SAS to work, and electrical power is delivered by the right AC and DC busses.

Two SAS channels are provided in both the pitch and yaw axes. Each channel acts on the respective control surface actuator. The output of the two channels is continuously compared and in the event of an excessive difference a computer deactivates both channels in the affected axis, triggering a light on the caution light panel.

The pitch and yaw SAS failure monitor circuits can be tested by using the monitor test switch on the SAS panel. An emergency disconnect lever, located immediately below the stick grip, disengages all SAS channels when momentarily depressed.

The pitch SAS provides the control functions for the IFFCC pitch commands and the pitch trim function. Total SAS authority is limited to 5° elevator trailing edge up and 2° elevator trailing edge down. A monitor circuit senses differential between the left and right channels and shuts off pitch SAS when the differential is excessive. A hydraulic or engine failure will not automatically result in SAS disengagement. However, the affected axis will disengage when a differential between channels is sensed. Control stick authority is more than sufficient to override an SAS-induced elevator displacement.

The yaw SAS performs three basic functions:

yaw rate damping with ±7° rudder authority, turn coordination with ±7° rudder authority and yaw trim with ±10° rudder authority.

The SAS authority is limited to ±10° below 240 KIAS and ±8° above 240 KIAS. The sideslip control is generated by the Inertial Navigation System (INS) or Heading Attitude Reference System (HARS) roll rate sensors, angle of attack (AoA) transmitter and yaw rate sensors.

A monitor circuit senses differential between the left and right channels and shuts off yaw SAS when the differential is excessive. A hydraulic or engine failure will not automatically result in SAS disengagement. However, the affected axis will disengage when a differential between channels is sensed. Rudder pedal authority is more than sufficient to override an SAS-induced rudder displacement. Below 240 KIAS, SAS can reduce the maximum obtainable rudder deflection from 25° to 15° in one direction. Above 240 KIAS, the full 8° of rudder deflection in either direction can always be obtained, regardless of SAS inputs.

Manual Reversion Flight Control System

The MRFCS is an emergency system for use when dual hydraulic failure is impending or has occurred. It is adequate for executing moderate manoeuvres, but landing should only be attempted under ideal conditions or when ejection is not possible.

Emergency transitions to manual reversion are automatic and instantaneous in pitch and yaw, with stick and pedal commands transmitted directly to the elevator and rudder surfaces through the actuators, which are in the hydraulic bypass mode.

Transitions in roll must be initiated. When 'MAN REVERSION' is selected, roll control is transferred from the ailerons to the aileron tabs. Selecting 'MAN REVERSION' also closes hydraulic shut-off valves, preventing unexpected return to hydraulic-powered flight control. Manual reversion trim is provided only in pitch.

Pitch MRFCS

Pitch transition to manual reversion occurs due to hydraulic pressure depletion. The same components are used for manual and hydraulic pitch control. As hydraulic pressure drops to 600–400psi, elevator control automatically changes from hydraulic to mechanical. Electrical control of the two elevator trim tabs is automatically achieved when both hydraulic power sources have dropped below 1,000–800psi. Artificial feel is retained.

Transition is reversible. Power control of the elevators is instantly restored as pressure at one (or both) of the actuators is increased above 700–900psi. Both elevator trim tabs trim to neutral when either pressure switch senses 1,000–1,200psi.

Yaw MRFCS

Yaw transition to manual reversion occurs due to hydraulic pressure depletion. The same mechanical elements are used for manual and hydraulic yaw control. As hydraulic pressure drops to 600–400psi, rudder control automatically changes from hydraulic to mechanical. Transition is reversible. Power control is instantly restored as pressure is increased to 700–900psi.

Roll MRFCS

To achieve roll control when hydraulic pressure is not present, the flight control mode switch must be set to 'MAN REVERSION'.

When 'MAN REVERSION' is selected, stick commands are disconnected from the aileron actuators and connected to the aileron tabs. In this tab drive mode, the aileron tabs fly the aileron surface to the position commanded by the stick. Feel at the stick is proportional to air loads on the tabs.

Aileron float-up transition

After loss of hydraulic pressure, the trailing edges of the ailerons float up to a position that is higher than the powered neutral position. Aileron float-up normally induces an aircraft pitch change which can be nose up or down depending on aircraft centre of gravity, elevator trim tab setting, power setting and flap position. The pitch change intensity varies and is dependent on aileron float-up rate, airspeed and altitude, and can range from -2.0g to +6.8g during transition.

To soften pitch onset, the aileron float-up rate is limited by damping in the actuators. The time for the ailerons to float up after hydraulic pressure loss/bleed-off is approximately four seconds.

Stall warning system

Stall warning stick shaker

Stick shaker operation is a function of the AoA (angle of attack) vane and AoA indicator and interlocks with the landing-gear position and flaps switch. The mechanical stick shaker is mounted on the control stick just above the protective boot. Stick shaker operation is triggered by an electronic switch located in the AoA indicator at 22.6 units.

Stick shaker operation requires the nose

BELOW A structural maintenance craftsman specialist drills out rivets while repairing battle damage on an A-10 extensively damaged by a handheld IR missile over Iraq. The aircraft's MRFCS was the only reason that the pilot made it back to base. *(USAF)*

generators and a caution annunciator light ('STALL SYS').

The Alpha Mach Computer computes discrete triggers for the steady peak-performance and chopped stall warning 600Hz tones. Both engine igniters initiate on the same discrete triggers as the stall chopped tone and continue one second after termination of the stall warning.

Tone activation is initiated by the Alpha Mach Computer as a function of the wing lift transducer signal and Mach computed from the pitot/static pneumatic inputs. The lift transducer is mounted on the front lower quadrant of the left wing.

A steady peak-performance tone is generated approximately two AoA units prior to stall and a chopped stall warning tone is generated approximately one AoA unit before stall. The chopped stall warning tone does not change in volume or frequency as AoA increases. Thus actual wing stall or its depth is not indicated by this system. The two headset tones are controlled by separate volume knobs on the stall warning control panel. The audio stall warning system is powered by the DC essential bus and is active as long as power is available. The leading edge slats are also controlled by the Alpha Mach Computer.

ABOVE The A-10 has a stall speed of around 120kt. As it approaches this portion of the flight envelope, or during conditions of an accelerated stall, a mechanical stick shaker gives the pilot tactile feedback of the impending departure, but only if the nose wheel is extended and the flap switch is in the down position.
(Steve Davies/ FJPhotography.com)

landing gear to be down or the flap switch to be in full down position and weight off the wheels. It provides mild agitation of the control stick 4 to 12kt prior to wing stall in 1g flight and is powered by the auxiliary DC essential bus.

Stall warning aural tones

The aural warning system consists of the Alpha Mach Computer, wing lift transducer, two-tone

RIGHT The A-10's Fowler flaps are set by a simple switch outboard of the left throttle. They automatically retract based on airspeed (in the region of 190kt).
(USAF)

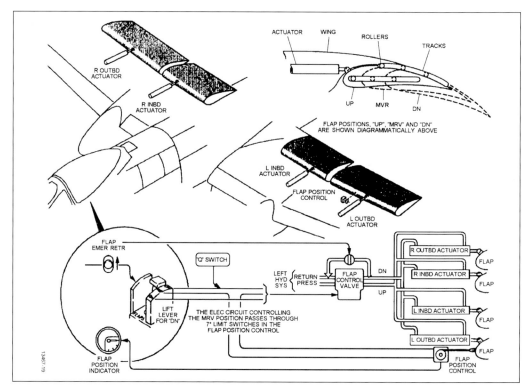

Secondary flight control system – flap, slat and speed brake

Flap

The aircraft is equipped with four wing trailing edge flaps. A cockpit control lever controls the flaps, commanding one of three positions: 0° ('UP'), 7° manoeuvre ('MVR') and 20° ('DN').

The flaps are individually supported and each flap is positioned by one hydraulic actuator and powered by the left hydraulic system. When extended, flaps hold position in the event of loss of flap system electrical and/or hydraulic power until commanded to go up by the flap emergency retract switch. On loss of the left hydraulic system, the flaps will be inoperative. When fully extended, aerodynamic forces will cause unpowered flaps to retract to less than 15° and manoeuvring flaps to retract to 0° if the emergency flap switch is activated.

In full 'UP' or 'DN', hydraulic pressure is retained in the selected position to eliminate flap creeping. During ground operations with the flap control set to 'MVR', the flaps may creep. The left outboard flap will cycle about the 7° position, and the other flap panels may assume varying positions. It may be necessary to recycle the flap lever to get all panels back to the 7° position.

Flaps will not extend and will automatically retract if the airspeed exceeds 185 to 210 KIAS. The flap control must be recycled through the 'UP' position, after the airspeed is below approximately 180 KIAS, in order to extend the flaps. When aircraft speed is reduced below approximately 190 KIAS (5–15 KIAS below auto retract speed), the flaps will automatically re-extend if the flap lever is in 'MVR' or 'DN'. Emergency flap retract capability is provided by an emergency flap switch on the emergency flight control panel. When activated, the switch shuts off pressure and opens the down lines to return. Aerodynamic forces drive the flaps up to a minimum position.

Slat

The slat system consists of movable two-position slat panels that are mounted on the inboard leading edge section of each wing. Slats are powered by the right hydraulic system. Electrical power for control is from the right DC bus.

The slats function automatically to improve high AoA airflow to the engines. The

BELOW The trailing edge of the flaps is almost in line with the leading edge of the engine intake lip, providing additional protection against the ingestion of foreign objects when taxiing, taking off and landing on unprepared airstrips. *(Steve Davies/ FJPhotography.com)*

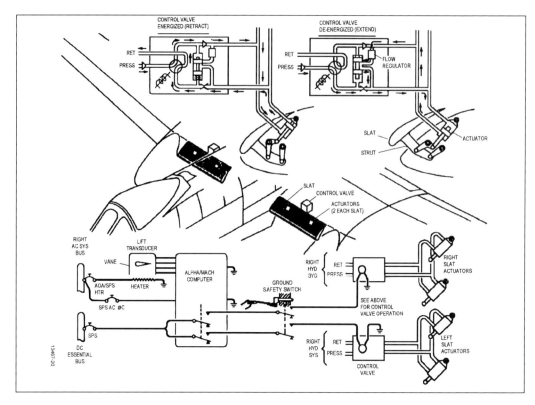

Emergency Stall Prevention System (ESPS) detects conditions that will lead to engine stall. Stall is determined in the ESPS system as a function of AoA and Mach. The AoA is measured by a lift transducer mounted on the lower side of the left wing leading edge. Mach is measured internally in the ESPS through the pitot static system. At a predetermined AoA and Mach, the slats extend. The ESPS is powered by the right AC bus.

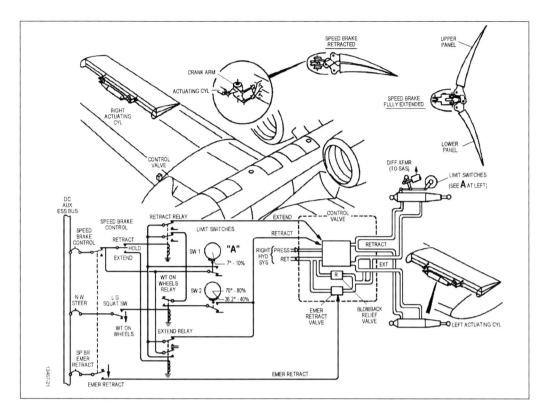

LEFT The clam-shell speed brakes are operated by the pilot using a thumb switch on the right throttle. Various logic is incorporated into them, and an aural warning 'Speed brake! Speed brake!' is sounded when the brakes are extended and the throttles are advanced to full military power. *(USAF)*

Speed brake

The speed brake surfaces and actuating mechanisms are integrated in the ailerons. The upper and lower surfaces of both ailerons open to act as speed brakes,

BELOW An 81st FS A-10A extends its speed brakes to reveal the squadron motto. The brakes will only extend to 80% of their full range of travel while the aircraft is airborne, allowing enough remaining travel for the split control surface to continue to operate as an aileron. *(USAF)*

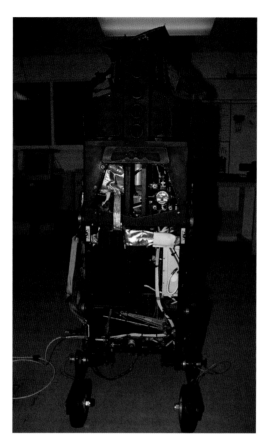

and open or close in approximately three seconds in flight.

A limit switch restricts the speed brakes to the 80% position during flight, and precludes holding positions of less than 10%. The WOW switch on the left MLG allows 100% deployment on the ground. If the aircraft becomes airborne with a speed brake position exceeding 80%, the speed brakes will not automatically retract to 80%. In this condition the speed brakes will only respond to retract commands initiated by the speed brake switch.

Automatic pitch trim compensation is provided by the IFFCC via pitch SAS for speed brake deployment. Automatic over-speed structural protection is provided by means of hydraulic relief action. The speed brakes blow back proportionally as air loads approach structural limits. Similarly, speed brake extend rate and travel is constrained at high speed.

With total loss of hydraulic power (right engine not rotating), aerodynamic forces will slowly close speed brakes to trail position. With right engine windmilling, and if commanded prior to engine failure, speed brakes will be held in position. If commanded after engine failure and engine is windmilling, partial extension (degree dependent on airspeed) can be expected. Closing speed brake switch or selecting 'SPD BK EMER RETR' will allow speed brakes to retract as hydraulic pressure is depleted.

With loss of electrical power the speed brakes will retract to the closed position hydraulically.

Ejection seat

The ACES II ejection seat is a dual initiated, fully automatic catapult rocket system. Three ejection modes are automatically selected. Mode 1 is a low-speed mode during which the parachute is deployed almost immediately after the seat departs the aircraft. Mode 2 is a high-speed mode during which a drogue chute is first deployed to slow the seat, followed by the deployment of the parachute. Mode 3 is a high-altitude mode in which the sequence of events is the same as Mode 2, except that man–seat separation and deployment of the parachute is delayed until a safe altitude is reached. Controls are provided to adjust seat height and lock shoulder harness.

Environmental system

The environmental system supplies temperature-controlled air for cockpit air conditioning and pressurisation. The system also provides service air for windshield and canopy defogging, windshield rain removal, canopy seal, anti-g suit pressurisation and external tank pressurisation.

The environmental system receives bleed air from the APU, an external source or from the engines. If the system becomes inoperative the cockpit can be ventilated by ram air.

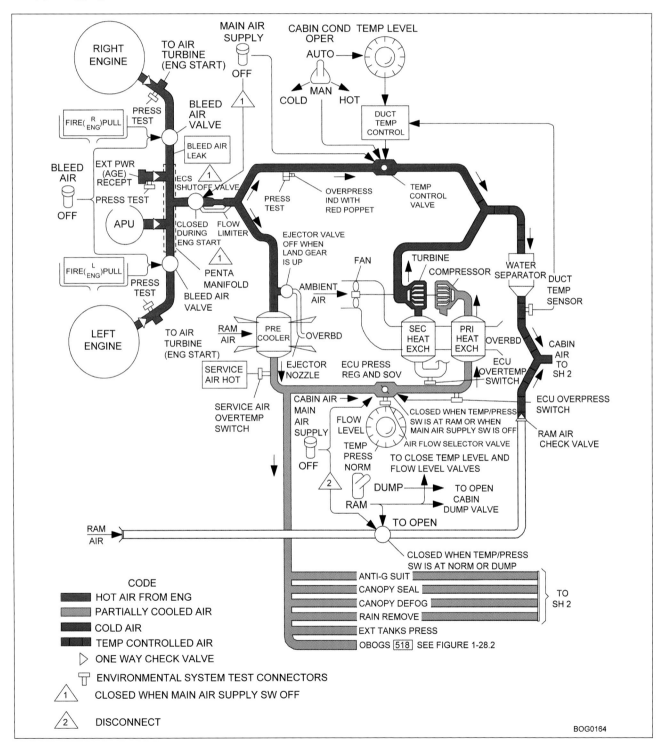

Chapter Six

Power for the A-10

The sound of the A-10 is as distinctive as the sound of a Chinook or Huey. The twin TF-34s may whine loudly as they push the draggy airframe through the air, but the engines have endeared themselves to the A-10 pilot as reliable and able to absorb the impact of enemy fire.

OPPOSITE The first A-10C Thunderbolt II sits on the ramp after its arrival at Moody Air Force Base, Georgia, on 7 August 2010. There had been plans to also re-engine the A-10, but in the event it still retained its trusted, if slightly underpowered, TF-34-GE-100As in late 2016. *(USAF)*

The A-10C is powered by two General Electric TF-34-GE-100A engines. Sea-level standard day maximum static thrust for each installed engine is approximately 8,900lb. Engine acceleration time from idle to maximum thrust is approximately ten seconds at sea level.

The same engine also powered the US Navy's Lockheed S-3 Viking (TF-34-GE-400A variant). General Electric claims that 'since entering service in the 1970s, 2,100 TF-34 engines have accumulated a total of more than 13 million engine flight hours spanning combat and peace time missions.' The A-10's GE-100 variant of the TF-34 entered service in 1976 and underwent hot section improvements during the 1980s.

The TF-34 incorporates a single-stage bypass fan and a 14-stage axial flow compressor. Because bypass air produces over 85% of engine thrust, engine fan speed is the best indication of thrust. Variable inlet guide vanes automatically modulate throughout the engine operating range, while an accessory gearbox drives a hydraulic pump, fuel pump and fuel control, oil pump and an electric generator. An air bleed for aircraft systems is provided.

Engine thrust droop results from differential expansion of the engine turbines and casings during transients from low- to high-thrust operation. The duration and extent of the thrust droop is dependent upon the rate/range of throttle movement.

Engine thrust droop

During turbine engine operation, heat expands the rotating and stationary components to normal operating dimensions and clearances. Engine thrust droop results from differential expansion of the engine turbines and casings during transients from low- to high-thrust operation.

An example of the worst condition would be a scramble take-off where take-off is accomplished shortly after engine start. Maximum droop occurs approximately ten seconds after the throttle is advanced from 'IDLE' to 'MAX'. After approximately four minutes of operation at maximum thrust, power output returns to normal.

Engine core lock

Engine core lock results when an engine is shut down because its rotating and stationary components do not contract at the same rates due to differences in material properties and differing exposure to cooling air. Temporary losses of clearances occur

RIGHT Consisting of fan, compressor, combustor and turbine sections, the TF34 generates 85% of its thrust from bypass air coming from the monstrous fan. *(USAF)*

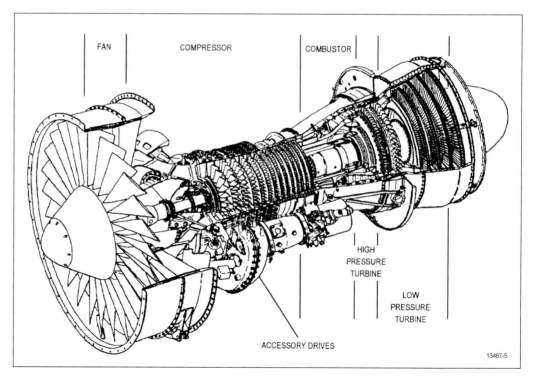

FAN   COMPRESSOR   COMBUSTOR

HIGH PRESSURE TURBINE

LOW PRESSURE TURBINE

ACCESSORY DRIVES

13467-5

until the temperatures of the components reach equilibrium.

Because of this characteristic, turbine engine shutdown procedures include operation for several minutes at a lower power setting to permit internal temperatures and clearances to stabilise.

Flameouts at high power and/or high-altitude conditions produce even greater thermal distress, because internal temperatures are hottest at high power settings and the external air is colder at high altitudes. A sudden engine shutdown under these conditions will cause increased thermal shock, exacerbating the loss of component clearance and alignment. Once core rotation stops, binding will prevent core rotation from resuming during subsequent APU-assisted restart attempts.

Turbine Engine Monitoring System

The TEMS provides a means of supporting the on-condition maintenance concept for the TF-34-100A. Information is provided to the system's electronic processor unit (EPU) automatically whenever the engine is operated.

On select A-10C aircraft the Improved Electronic Processor Unit (IEPU) is a form, fit, function replacement for the existing EPU. The IEPU monitors engine and airframe-mounted sensors and monitors, via the aircraft 1553 Avionics 1 data bus, aircraft performance parameters. The IEPU OFP (operational flight program) determines and records aircraft structural events that are retrieved for later analysis. Engine-related performance and event data is retrieved and processed by the Comprehensive Engine and Trending Acquisition Database (CETADS) system.

Engine oil system

The engine oil system is self-contained and all the oil supplied is used for lubrication and cooling. Usable oil capacity is 5.6 quarts, and maximum oil consumption is 0.5 pints per hour. An oil pressure indicator and an independent light on the caution light panel monitor oil pressure of each engine.

Engine fuel system

The engine fuel system provides fuel required for combustion, controls engine variable geometry actuation and provides engine oil cooling.

Fuel is supplied to the engine fuel pumps, where it is pressurised and directed to the fuel control. From the fuel control metered fuel passes through the engine oil cooler to the distribution valve.

RIGHT A crew chief conducts post-flight operations on an A-10C, installing engine covers to prevent FOD entering the TF-34's massive fans. *(USAF)*

BELOW Power from the engines is controlled by the two throttles mounted on the left cockpit console. Ahead of the throttles are fuel and ignition controls, allowing the pilot to isolate an engine if required or conduct an air or ground restart following a flameout or start problem. *(USAF)*

The engine fuel control is a hydro-mechanical type that modulates fuel flow to maintain a constant core speed, as called for by throttle position. An electrical control unit regulates fuel flow at maximum power to maintain interstage turbine temperature (ITT) limits.

The fuel control also prevents compressor discharge pressure from exceeding the structural limits of the compressor. At sea level static, this limit is normally encountered at maximum power when engine inlet temperature is 0°F or colder. The limit can also be encountered on a standard day at sea level above approximately 330kt. In this case it will not be possible to obtain rated ITT.

The fuel control unit automatically adjusts the position of the compressor inlet guide vanes and the first five stator stages to prevent compressor stall. It does not require electrical power, but the ITT control unit is powered by the auxiliary AC essential bus.

Throttles

A mechanical throttle controls the operation of each engine. Each throttle has three positive stop positions, labelled 'OFF', 'IDLE' and 'MAX'. To move from 'OFF' to 'IDLE' the throttle is raised and moved forward to the first stop position. To move to 'OFF' the throttle is retarded to the 'IDLE' stop, then raised and moved aft to 'OFF'. The DC fuel pump is energised when either throttle is positioned to 'IDLE' or above and there is no pressure from the left main tank boost pump.

When the throttle is at the 'IDLE' stop, the following actions take place provided engine

core rpm is below 56% and electrical power and an air source are available:

- Air turbine start (ATS) valve opens, causing the 'ENG START CYCLE' light to come on.
- Environmental control system (ECS) shut-off valve closes.
- Both engine bleed air shut-off valves open.
- Ignition is supplied to the engine.
- Fuel is supplied when engine rotation starts.
- DC fuel pump is energised if there is no fuel pressure from the left main tank boost pump.

Engine speed is normally controlled by the throttle. Under certain flight conditions the engine fuel control overrides the throttle to protect the engine from over-temperature, over-pressure and compressor stall.

Throttle friction for both throttles is controlled by means of the friction control located on the throttle quadrant.

Engine ignition system

Ignition is supplied by two ignitors in each engine. The ignition ignitors are powered by the AC essential bus and actuated by DC-powered relays.

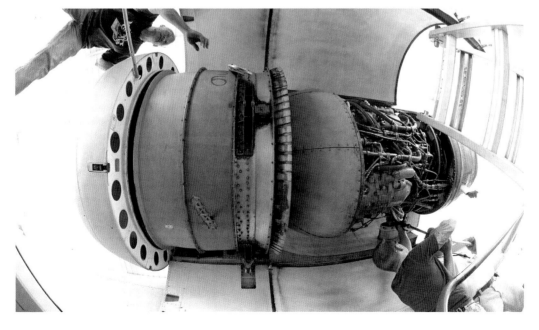

LEFT Air Force reservists remove a TF-34 from an A-10 at Whiteman Air Force Base, Missouri. The occasion was momentous because this particular engine had set a 442nd Fighter Wing record – staying on the same A-10 for ten years, accumulating 3,464.4 hours in the process. *(USAF)*

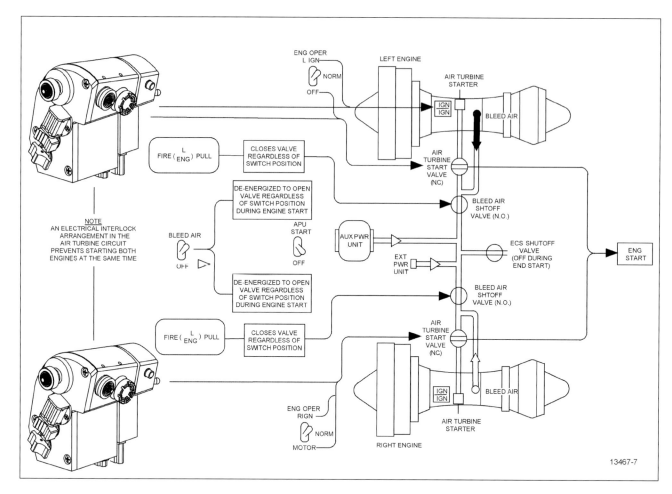

The figure contains the following labels:

ENG OPER L IGN — NORM — OFF

LEFT ENGINE

AIR TURBINE STARTER

IGN / IGN

BLEED AIR

FIRE (L ENG) PULL — CLOSES VALVE REGARDLESS OF SWITCH POSITION

AIR TURBINE START VALVE (NC)

BLEED AIR SHTOFF VALVE (N.O.)

DE-ENERGIZED TO OPEN VALVE REGARDLESS OF SWITCH POSITION DURING ENGINE START

APU START — OFF

NOTE
AN ELECTRICAL INTERLOCK ARRANGEMENT IN THE AIR TURBINE CIRCUIT PREVENTS STARTING BOTH ENGINES AT THE SAME TIME

BLEED AIR — OFF

AUX PWR UNIT

EXT PWR UNIT

ECS SHUTOFF VALVE (OFF DURING END START)

ENG START

DE-ENERGIZED TO OPEN VALVE REGARDLESS OF SWITCH POSITION DURING ENGINE START

BLEED AIR SHTOFF VALVE (N.O.)

FIRE (L ENG) PULL — CLOSES VALVE REGARDLESS OF SWITCH POSITION

AIR TURBINE START VALVE (NC)

BLEED AIR

ENG OPER RIGN — NORM — MOTOR

AIR TURBINE STARTER

IGN / IGN

RIGHT ENGINE

13467-7

ABOVE Both engines produce bleed air used by the environmental control system. Note how dedicated engine and APU fire handles automatically shut off bleed air when pulled. *(USAF)*

Bleed air system

Bleed air from each engine, from the APU and from a ground receptacle are routed to a common manifold. The bleed air supply system furnishes air for the following:

- Engine starter system.
- Environmental control system.
- Windshield rain removal and wash system.
- Canopy defog system.
- Canopy seal.
- Anti-g suit.
- External tank pressurisation.
- On-board oxygen generating system (OBOGS).

Bleed air supplied from the engines is controlled by a shut-off valve adjacent to each engine. Both valves are opened or closed simultaneously by the bleed air switch.

A temperature sensor is provided adjacent to the manifold for bleed air leak detection. The bleed air leak detection system is powered by the auxiliary AC essential bus.

Engine start system

Engine starts require low-pressure air to power the ATS (air turbine start) unit mounted on the engine. Air may be obtained from the following sources:

- APU.
- Crossbleed air from an operating engine (85% core rpm minimum).
- External pneumatic power unit.

Air from any of these sources is ducted through the bleed air shut-off valves to the ATS valves.

The throttle must be in 'IDLE' to obtain starter-assisted engine starts. If the throttle is moved above 'IDLE', the bleed air to the starter

will be shut off. The electrical circuits controlling the two ATS valves are interlocked to prevent both valves being opened at the same time, and insufficient air pressure is available to start both engines simultaneously.

After the start is complete the ATS valve is closed (automatically or manually) to prevent overspeeding of the ATS, and the 'ENG START CYCLE' light goes off. During the start, the ECS is shut off automatically to eliminate bleed air drain during the start cycle. Electrical power for starting the engines may be obtained from an external AC power unit, aircraft battery and inverter, or APU generator.

The aircraft contains an automatic engine starting system. Automatic engine starting will be initiated when the throttle is moved to 'IDLE', provided the engine core rpm is below 56% and electrical power and an air source are available. The following events occur:

■ ATS valve opens, allowing engine to rotate.
■ ECS shut-off valve closes.

ABOVE Airmen work together to remove a low-pressure turbine from a TF-34 engine. The men occupy the career field known as 'aerospace propulsion journeymen'. *(USAF)*

■ Both engine bleed air shut-off valves open.
■ Ignition is supplied for a minimum of 30 seconds.
■ Fuel is provided after engine starts to rotate.
■ ATS valve closes within 10 seconds after engine reaches 56% core rpm
■ ECS valve opens within 10 seconds after engine reaches 56% core rpm.
■ Both engine bleed air shut-off valves close after engine reaches 56% core rpm.

Fire-extinguishing system

A fire-extinguishing system is available to both engines and to the APU compartment/area. It consists of fire extinguishing agent stored in two independently actuated pressurised bottles located in the fuselage.

Either bottle may be discharged to either engine nacelle or the APU compartment area by pulling the appropriate fire handle and actuating the discharge switch.

The fire-extinguishing system operates on battery bus power. However, fire detection and fuel/bleed air shut-off functions require auxiliary DC essential and DC essential bus power.

Fire detection system

Fire detection is provided for in both engine nacelles and in the APU area by continuous temperature-sensitive elements. The fire warning light in the applicable left or right engine fire handle will come on when the entire sensor element detects fire/overheat conditions.

The APU fire and overheat system is similar to the engine fire system except that the warning light is in the APU fire handle. The APU fire detection includes coverage for the adjacent hydraulic, fuel, electrical, flight control and environmental control subsystems equipment installed in the fuselage between the fuel tank aft bulkhead and the frame aft of the APU.

Both systems are powered by the auxiliary DC essential bus.

Auxiliary power unit

The APU supplies air for engine starting, drives a generator for aircraft electrical power and can drive a hydraulic pump to pressurise the aircraft hydraulic system for ground maintenance functions. The unit is

BELOW A crew chief inspects the engine intake lip and cowling for cracks during a Red Flag-Alaska deployment to Eielson Air Force Base, Alaska. When units deploy to the exercise, maintainers must perform all aircraft maintenance and operate self-sufficiently, just as they would in a wartime environment. *(USAF)*

located in the aft fuselage between the engines and is provided with safety devices that shut down the APU when certain operating limitations are exceeded.

Fuel for APU starting is supplied by the DC fuel pump, and APU controls are powered by the DC essential bus. APU starting requires only DC essential bus power and a fuel supply.

When the APU start switch is positioned to 'START', the DC essential bus power operates the DC fuel pump, opens the APU fuel valve (aft fuel tank-mounted), and energises the APU starter. The starter rotates the APU compressor and, at approximately 10% rpm, the APU fuel valve (APU-mounted) opens and fuel and ignition are supplied to the APU. Acceleration of the APU continues until at approximately 60% rpm the starter disengages. At approximately 95% rpm ignition is terminated and the APU is self-sustaining.

APU speed and turbine discharge temperature are automatically controlled. The APU will stabilise at 100% (±3%) rpm in approximately 60 seconds. APU starts can be made up to an altitude of 15,000ft (most cases up to 20,000ft) and the APU output will be sufficient to start an engine up to an altitude of 10,000ft (most cases up to 15,000ft). The APU will operate during negative g conditions for approximately ten seconds.

APU will automatically shut down during ground operation if the APU exhaust gas temperature is excessive, APU rpm is excessive, APU oil pressure is low or the APU fire warning system is activated.

BELOW The A-10's APU exhaust is located on the port side, beneath the engine cowling. The APU gives the A-10 significant flexibility to operate in austere locations, not least because it means it is less dependent on aerospace ground equipment to operate. *(Steve Davies/ FJPhotography.com)*

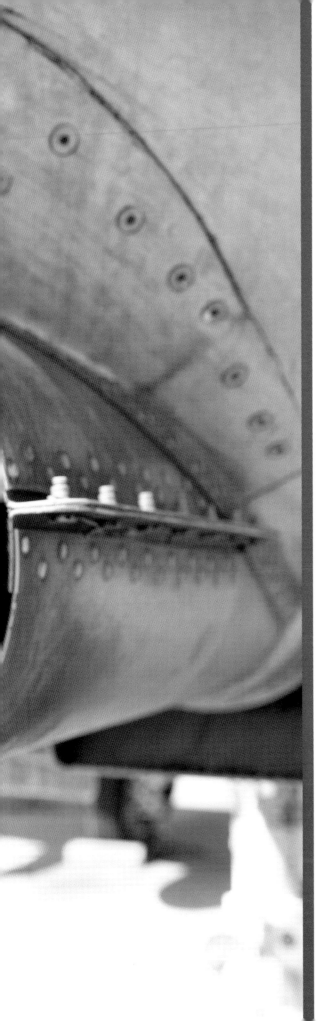

Chapter Seven

A-10C firepower

Today's A-10C has some of the same precision strike weapons and sensors as an F-15E Strike Eagle or F-16CM Viper, making it deadlier than ever before and less dependent on other platforms to find and kill its quarry. It's a far cry from the original A-10A, which was armed almost exclusively with 'dumb' or unguided weapons intended to be delivered visually.

OPPOSITE The seven-barrelled Avenger takes pride of place at the front of the Warthog. Displaced slightly to port, it fires gargantuan 30mm shells the size of a milk bottle (for those who remember such antiquities!). *(Steve Davies/ FJPhotography.com)*

Since entering service, the A-10 has received a number of important upgrades to make it more deadly. These include the Pave Penny laser spot tracker, the AGM-65 Maverick fire-and-forget missile (in both EO and IR versions), an EGI navigation system, target pods and a Digital Stores Management System (DSMS) to bind everything together. The DSMS is an often-overlooked element of the A-10C upgrade programme, but it is important because it allows the pilot to pre-load weapons release profiles and fuse settings (things that would have been done by switches and on the fly in the A-10A), therefore reducing both the time spent 'heads down' and the possibility of switch errors.

With the advent of inertially aided munition (IAM), best characterised by the JDAM series of weapons, today's C-model Hog pilot can fly and attack in any weather using either pre-planned coordinates, those passed from another asset, or those generated in real time by the target pod, HUD or moving map display. What's more, he can engage a single target in one pass, or engage multiple targets using side-by-side, tandem or diamond pattern releases of multiple IAMs in a single pass.

The most recent addition to the A-10 armoury, starting in June 2016, is the laser-guided rocket – the Advanced Precision Kill Weapon System (APKWS), which is being fielded by A-10s in Afghanistan at time of writing (late 2016).

While this chapter discusses most, but not all, of the A-10C's armoury, Appendix D provides a comprehensive list of stores cleared for use by the aircraft.

GAU-8/A

Throughout all the A-10's upgrades, one thing has remained constant: the awesome 30mm GAU-8/A Avenger cannon. The Avenger is a seven-barrel Gatling weapon weighing 679lb. It has a double-ended linkless feed system with a capacity for up to 1,174 rounds of percussion-primed ammunition. The gun system retains all spent cases or dud rounds. The installation of the gun system is such that it positions the firing barrel approximately on the aircraft centreline. The gun muzzle protrudes at the fuselage nose with the gun mechanism located under the cockpit and the ammunition drum located in the area just behind the cockpit. Firing rate is up to 3,900 rounds per minute.

The gun is driven by a gearbox with two separately controlled hydraulic drive motors and control valves mounted on the support structure between the ammunition storage system. It is connected by a mechanical transmission to the A/A 49E-6 armament subsystem, comprised of the ammunition storage system, feed and drive.

The GAU-8/A is boresighted to 41 milliradians

ABOVE Looking down the barrel of death – the Avenger cannon emits a burping sound as 30mm rounds leave its seven rotating barrels in a hurry (in fact, they only leave one barrel at a time – the top one). The weapon is fed with linkless ammunition and the spent shell casings are retained for recycling. *(Steve Davies/ FJPhotography.com)*

RIGHT Below and to the aft, a scoop hoovers up some of the gas that is emitted when the gun fires, helping to prevent secondary gun gas ignition in which the gas could ignite, starving the two TF-34s of oxygen to burn. *(Steve Davies/ FJPhotography.com)*

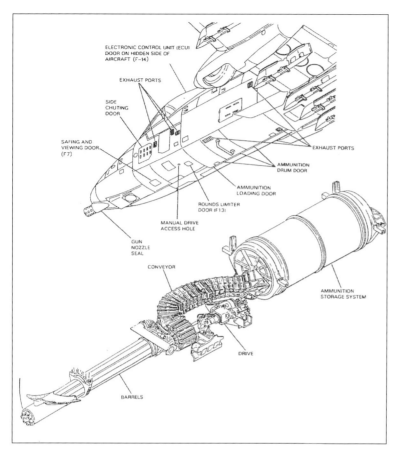

ELECTRONIC CONTROL UNIT (ECU)
DOOR ON HIDDEN SIDE OF
AIRCRAFT (F-14)

EXHAUST PORTS

SIDE
CHUTING
DOOR

SAFING AND
VIEWING DOOR
(F7)

EXHAUST PORTS

AMMUNITION
DRUM DOOR

AMMUNITION
LOADING DOOR

ROUNDS LIMITER
DOOR (F13)

MANUAL DRIVE
ACCESS HOLE

GUN
NOZZLE
SEAL

CONVEYOR

AMMUNITION
STORAGE SYSTEM

DRIVE

BARRELS

below zero sight line, and is harmonised for 4,000ft slant range under the following conditions: 29,700lb aircraft; 30° dive; and 250 KIAS.

General Electric beat designs from both

Philco Ford and famous Swiss manufacturer Oerlikon to win the competition to equip the A-10 with its famous gun. From the start, the Air Force took very seriously the importance of the gun, ensuring that both it and its ammunition had dedicated development programmes that involved at least two subcontractors.

In April 1971 the Air Force issued an RFP for competitive prototype development of a CAS gun system. Of the respondents, GE and Philco Ford were selected to compete for the contract.

In parallel, the Air Force also looked at Oerlikon's offering, the 304RK 30mm weapon, which had already been in operational service for some ten years on the SAAB J37 Viggen, and for which Vought had proposed a twin installation on the A-7D Corsair II. The Swiss weapon was seen as having too low a rate of fire, and there were also concerns over its reliability, but the Air Force hedged its bets and, in April 1973, designated the weapon the GAU-9/A and committed to selecting it as an alternative in the event that GE and Philco Ford were unable to produce anything better. In the event, GE beat Philco Ford hands down, delivering a design so good that it left the GAU-9/A in its wake.

Of course, the Avenger needs ammunition, and that comes in the form of inert target practice rounds for peacetime training, or

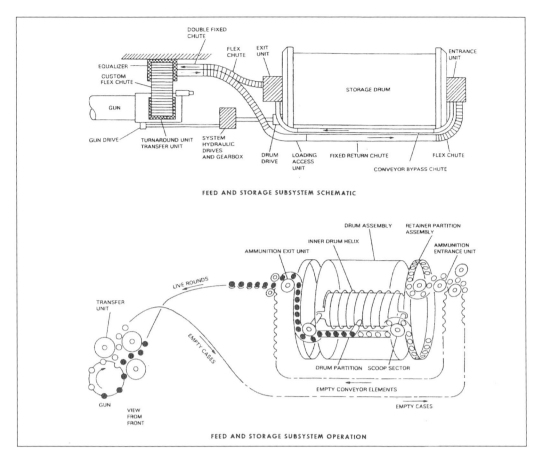

FEED AND STORAGE SUBSYSTEM SCHEMATIC

FEED AND STORAGE SUBSYSTEM OPERATION

high-explosive incendiary and armour-piercing incendiary rounds for combat. An armour-piercing incendiary round with a depleted uranium penetrator (also known as DU) is also used when heavily armoured targets are to be taken out. The latter is controversial due to its radioactivity, and the fact that once expended there is no way to know where the round (or shards of it) will end up. The United States conducted testing in the 1970s which concluded that there was no significant environmental or medical impact from expended DU rounds, but today some assert that exposure to expended DU rounds in the Middle East and Balkans has resulted in elevated rates of life-threatening illness.

Sensors

The A-10C carries the AAQ-33 Sniper SE advanced targeting pod and AAQ-28 Litening targeting pod. Sniper provides better image quality and capabilities than the Litening pod, but both are highly capable and give the Hog pilot the ability to stand off from the target,

plan an attack, then come back in and execute it autonomously.

Lockheed Martin, which makes the Sniper, describes it as 'an electro-optical targeting system in a single, lightweight pod that is

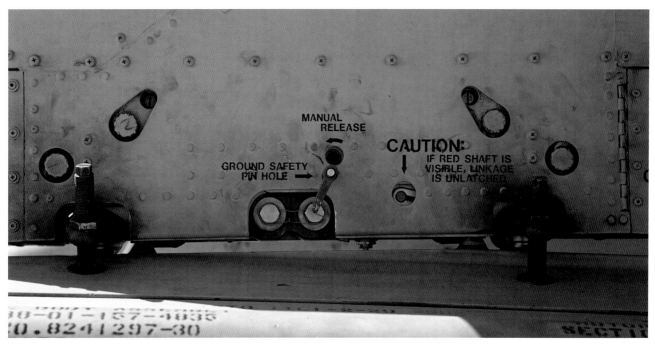

ABOVE The MAU series of ejector racks act as the interface between pylon and store or pylon and launcher. This close-up of a MAU-40 provides a clear view of the very simple design of its sway braces. *(Steve Davies/FJPhotography.com)*

compatible with the latest precision-guided weapons for detecting, identifying and engaging multiple moving and fixed targets in air-to-air and air-to-ground engagements. In addition to fulfilling strike mission requirements, Sniper is changing the way armed forces operate in theater to meet the challenges of non-traditional intelligence, surveillance and reconnaissance (NTISR). With capabilities including long-range target detection and identification and continuous stabilised surveillance, Sniper enables aircrews to find and destroy targets outside of jet noise ranges. Sniper's two-way video datalink for communicating with forward-deployed forces, superior imagery, and weapon quality coordinates allow pilots to make rapid targeting decisions.'

While the A-10 started life with the AAS-35(V) Pave Penny pod as a means to detect a coded laser pulse on the battlefield, the integration of true target pods – featuring EO and IR video, and capabilities such as moving-target tracking – has ushered in an autonomous precision strike attack that those running the A-X programme probably could not have imagined.

Armament pylons and launchers

The A-10 has 11 external pylon stations. The seven inboard stations (3 through 9) house the MAU-40/A ejector rack and are capable of multiple bomb loadings. The four outboard pylons (1, 2, 10 and 11) carry the MAU-50/A ejector rack.

The TER 9/A and BRU-42LS are auxiliary suspension racks (triple ejection racks) used to increase the number of munitions the A-10 can carry. A TER can carry and sequentially eject up to three stores, each weighing up to 1,000lb and measuring 16in in diameter.

The LAU-88/A, LAU-88A/A and LAU-117(V)1/A launchers are designed to carry, control and launch AGM-65 missiles from aircraft stations 3 and 9. The LAU-131 and LAU-68 are used to carry rocket pods.

The A-10's air-to-air missile launcher system provides means for selection, arming and launch of AIM-9 Sidewinder missiles. It is configured to accommodate a Dual Rail Adapter (DRA) with LAU-105 launchers loaded with missiles on station 1 and/or station 11, although it is traditional for station 11 to carry the AIM-9s and station 1 to be reserved for an ECM pod.

The MXU-648 travel pod is used to carry personal equipment during deployments from one location to another.

ABOVE AND BELOW It's the nature of the 422nd TES's work – developing operational tactics, techniques and procedures – that the squadron conducts more live-fire weapons testing than any other A-10 unit. Here, a 'Green Bats' A-10C sits fully loaded on the ramp at Nellis, sunshade installed in the cockpit to keep the temperature below 35°C as it awaits the arrival of its pilot. It carries live Mk 82s, GBU-38s, rockets and GBU-12s. The Mavericks and Sidewinders are the only inert or captive-carry stores loaded. *(Steve Davies/FJPhotography.com)*

Training and fuel tanks

A range of captive carry stores can be hauled aloft by the A-10C, including CATM-65 and TGM-65 training rounds for Maverick missiles, WTU-16 practice rockets, captive CAP-9 Sidewinders and inert BDU-50 (Mk 84 LDGP) stores.

In addition, the SUU-20 bomb dispenser provides the A-10 with an externally mounted pod from which to shoot practice rockets and drop BDU-33 practice bombs. The dispenser is designed to carry six BDU-33s in a recessed open bay and held in individual bomb ejector racks by retention arms, swaybraces and ejector pistons.

The BDU-33 is intended to approximately mimic the Mk 82 LDGP (Low-Drag General Purpose) bomb, and has a teardrop-shaped body cast in metal, with a hollow round signal cavity running lengthwise through the centre. A conical fin assembly, with a cruciform-type fin, is roll-crimped into two grooves in the aft end of the bomb body. The store contains a small smoke charge to help spot it as it impacts the ground.

For peacetime operations in instrumented range spaces, an Airborne Instrumentation System pod can be carried in place of an AIM-9. When a rangeless pod is required (*eg* to be used outside an instrumented training range), the AN/ASQ-T50 TSTS pod incorporates a data link to share positional and weapons data with other similarly equipped aircraft.

The 600-gallon FT-600 fuel tank can be carried on the centreline station (6) and on the two inboard stations (5 and 7). A maximum of three tanks can be carried.

Air-to-ground: guided

JDAM

The Joint Direct Attack Munition (JDAM) is a modular kit used to convert Low Drag General Purpose (LDGP) unguided bombs into all-weather, precision strike weapons. It is referred to formally as an inertially aided munition, or IAM. IAMs allow the Hog pilot to engage targets from 5,000ft above the ground and higher, according to an unclassified A-10 capabilities brief.

JDAM incorporates a new tail section (containing an inertial navigational system and a global positioning system guidance control unit) with an LDGP munition of 500lb (Mk 82), 1,000lb (Mk 83) or 2,000lb (Mk 84) class. Once converted, the designation of the weapon becomes GBU-38 (Mk 82), GBU-32 (Mk 83) and GBU-31 (Mk 84).

The USAF stocks the GBU-38 and -31, but not the GBU-32 (this is used by the US Navy). The GBU-31 also comes in a range of penetrator variants for use against hardened and buried targets, although so-called 'bunker busting' JDAMs tend to be carried by fast jets and heavy bombers that can release the weapon from high altitude and impart the required kinetic energy needed for the bomb to penetrate the target.

A dual-mode 500lb JDAM known as the Laser JDAM (GBU-54) gives the A-10 pilot the ability to engage targets in instances where the weather may be marginal, or where the target is obscured

by smoke. In these situations, the weapon will seek out the coded laser of the Litening or Sniper pod, but revert to GPS guidance if the laser signal is unavailable or interrupted. The LJDAM has also been used to strike targets beneath a cloud layer, with a ground-based designator lasing the target during the terminal phase of the bomb's fall to earth.

WCMD

The CBU-103 and CBU-105 are wind-corrected munitions dispensers (WCMD): cluster munitions equipped with a guidance and steering kit similar to JDAM, allowing the weapon to be released over the target from medium altitude without fear of it being blown adrift by the prevailing winds aloft.

The CBU-103 is the WCMD version of the CBU-87 CEM (see below), while the CBU-105

ABOVE LEFT AND ABOVE The GBU-38 JDAM is a 500lb weapon with dual INS and GPS guidance. Most useful against fixed or static targets, multiple GBU-38s can be dropped by an A-10 against multiple targets in a single pass. Note the strake kit attached to the nose of the bomb to provide additional aerodynamic stability during its fall to earth. *(USAF)*

is the WCMD version of the CBU-97 SFW (see below).

Laser Guided Bomb (LGB)

The Paveway series of laser guided bombs has long been in the A-10 inventory. The first series GBU-10C Paveway I is a 2,000lb Mk 84 fitted with a seeker head guidance and steering kit, and a pop-out tail fin kit. The more modern GBU-12 Paveway III is a 500lb Mk 82 bomb similarly modified. In contrast to the PWI's 'bang bang' control, whereby the steering fins

BELOW An A-10C makes the first-ever drop of a Laser Joint Direct Attack Munition, or LJDAM, also known as the GBU-54. The aircraft belongs to the 40th Flight Test Squadron at Eglin Air Force Base, Florida. *(USAF)*

LEFT The GBU-12 Paveway III weapon features pop-out fins at the rear (which deploy when the weapon is released) and a guidance and steering module attached to the front, both of which are mated to a Mk 82 LDGP bomb. The GBU-12 has been phenomenally successful, not only as employed by the A-10 community but also in the hands of many other Fighter aviation communities in the US and abroad. *(Steve Davies/FJPhotography.com)*

ABOVE AND BELOW An A-10C of the 188th Fighter Wing, Arkansas Air National Guard, lets loose an AGM-65 Maverick over the ranges near Davis-Monthan Air Force Base, Arizona. The Maverick is loaded on to the LAU-88/A, LAU-88A/A and LAU-117(V)1/A launchers, and can be carried on triple ejector racks, although this configuration is rarely seen. *(USAF [above and below left] and Steve Davies/FJPhotography.com [below right])*

can only be commanded to either deflect to their full range of travel or remain in the neutral position, the PWIII features graduated control fin movements that conserve energy and improve the bomb's stand-off range, CEP and kinetic impact potential.

The GBU-12 became the weapon of choice against moving and fleeting targets during Operations Enduring Freedom and Iraqi Freedom.

EO/IR guided

The Maverick fire-and-forget missile entered production after the A-10 had been purchased, but the two were always intended to go together.

The missile comes in a range of variants – AGM-65D, G, H and K being the ones employed by the A-10 – and differ in their use of warhead and seeker. For example, the AGM-65D has an imaging IR seeker, but the AGM-65G has an improved IIR seeker and a bigger warhead. The AGM-65H has a charge-coupled device EO seeker, while the AGM-65K has the same CCD seeker but the heavier warhead of the G-model Maverick.

The missile displays its seeker view to the pilot via a video feed, allowing him to find and identify a target, then command a lock-on of the missile seeker. Once launched, the missile guides itself to the target.

At night, the IR variants of the missile provided a 'poor man's' forward looking infrared (FLIR) to the A-10 community prior to the arrival of the Litening and Sniper target pods.

Advanced Precision Kill Weapon System (APKWS)

The APKWS weapon is a 2.75in rocket fielded in June 2016. The rocket features a guidance nose cone with a 40-degree field of view, and pop-out fins to steer the rocket. The pilot lases the target using the Sniper or Litening pod, and the rockets lock on to the reflected energy of the laser pulse after launch, steering themselves to the target accordingly.

Air-to-ground: unguided

Miscellaneous

When resupply of allied ground forces is required, the CTU-2/A resupply container can be used. The parachute-retarded tube can

be loaded with any equipment that fits, up to a maximum weight of 500lb.

LDGP, AIR, SE and HD

The Low-Drag General Purpose, Air Inflatable Retard (AIR), Snake Eye and High Drag variants of the Mk 82 500lb and Mk 84 2,000lb bombs have all been familiar stores in the inventory of the A-10. Today only the LDGP and HD variants remain in service.

From initial entry to service all the way through to the most recent conflicts around the globe, these stores have provided the Hog pilot with flexible, dependable and simple weapons effects in the face of increasing battlefield sophistication.

Rockets

The A-10C employs 2.75in rockets in WP (white phosphorous), HE (high explosive), and illumination (M257) versions. It can do so using a continuously computed impact point reticule in the HUD, or using a continuously computed release point mode against distant targets.

The rockets can be carried in a range of different pods, in single or triple carriage configurations.

Illumination

The SUU-25 flare launcher carries eight parachute-retarded LUU-2 flares and is used to provide illumination over the battlefield from stand-off ranges.

Cluster weapons

The CBU-87 Combined Effects Munition and the CBU-97 Sensor Fused Weapon remain components in the A-10 weapons inventory despite growing international distaste for cluster munitions, although the CBU-97 has been designed with a very low rate of failure in mind and features a safety failsafe. Both are in the 1,000lb class of weapons.

The CBU-87 comprises a SUU-65B canister containing 202 BLU-97 bomblets. It is designed for use against armour, soft-skinned targets and personnel, so each bomblet has a shaped charge, a zirconium ring to generate incendiary effects, and a fragmentation case.

The CBU-97 is designed for use against armour and contains ten BLU-108 sub-munitions housed in a SUU-66/B dispenser.

OPPOSITE A 66th Weapons Squadron A-10C leaves behind it a mini mushroom cloud, the end result of a well-placed Mk 82 LDGP bomb. It's interesting to note that, despite the availability of smart weapons to the Hog pilot, sometimes it's the dumb munitions like rockets and airburst Mk 82s that are the go-to weapon. *(USAF)*

Each BLU-108 contains four 'skeets' – charges equipped with an IR and laser sensor that scans the scene below for armoured targets such as tanks and armoured personnel carriers, finds and identifies its target and then fires an explosively formed penetrator into it.

ABOVE The rocket pod, like this seven-tube LAU-131, provides the A-10 with a multitude of options – HE rounds, illumination or parachute illumination, smoke and WP (white phosphorous). It's rare to see a Hog without at least one LAU pod. *(Steve Davies/FJPhotography.com)*

Air-to-air

The idea of the A-10 operating in the air-to-air sphere may seem ridiculous, but, like its namesake, the Warthog has a fearsome reputation for defending itself. It may be energy limited, but it has one good turn in it, and it can use that turn to get inside the turn circle of any modern-day fighter or to cause an overshoot. When either of these happens it can bring the massive firepower of the Avenger to bear, or squeeze off a Sidewinder missile or two. When confronted with battlefield helicopters or opposing CAS platforms (such as the Su-25 Frogfoot), the A-10 pilot may actually choose to go on the offensive.

The AIM-9, of which up to four can be carried, is a fire-and-forget missile that guides on to a heat source. The missile seeker's field of view is presented in the HUD, and the pilot can fly this FOV circle over the target and uncage the missile seeker, allowing it to gimbal and follow the heat source. Alternatively he can

BELOW Mounted on a Dual Rail Adapter (DRA), LAU-105 launchers give the A-10 the ability to carry two AIM-9 Sidewinders on station 1 and/or station 11. *(Steve Davies/ FJPhotography.com)*

uncage the seeker without a lock, sending the seeker head into a circular scan pattern that allows it to lock on to the first heat source it detects. The missile generates a growl in the pilot's headset, rising to a high-pitch shrill when the seeker head has detected a heat source, giving the pilot the cue he needs to 'hammer down on the pickle button' and send the missile towards its target.

For a gun engagement, the LASTE programme added important symbology to the HUD, including a 'funnel' indicator that uses stadiametric ranging based on a target wingspan setting entered by the pilot and is

useful against crossing targets. The funnel gives the pilot a lead-angle computation that allows him to pull 'lead' ahead of the target, keeping the target aircraft wingspan touching the edge of the funnel to ensure the 30mm rounds impact the target. LASTE also added the multiple reference gun-sight display, which provides an alternative to the funnel in situations where the target has more of a frontal or rear aspect, and uses target length and velocity to create lead-angle solutions for the pilot.

Countermeasures

To protect itself, the A-10C has a fairly sophisticated range of defensive equipment. It boasts both a radar warning receiver for detection and classification of radar threats, and a fully integrated Common Missile Warning System (CMWS) that detects laser pulses and the UV radiation of missile exhaust plumes. These devices all provide warnings – aural and visual – to alert the pilot to the threat. On the left outboard wing pylon, the Hog usually carries an ALQ-131(A) countermeasures pod that is quoted as being the most advanced in the USAF's combat air force (CAF), and which automatically jams threat radars based on the

threat level they pose. The pilot can set the pod to prioritise jamming efforts against either SAM or airborne systems, as required.

Completing the defensive suite is a countermeasure/ (chaff and flare) program that is also touted as the most advanced of all USAF legacy fighters. The system, which can be activated manually or automatically, comprises preset programmes for chaff and flare dispensing that the pilot can select from, based on the threat he is most likely to encounter. Alternatively, he can leave the system to automatically select the best dispensing programme based on the data being fed to it by the RWR (radar warning receiver), ALQ-131 and CMWS. He can also manually create a programme to specify burst count and interval, and salvo count and interval.

The A-10 carries more chaff and flares than any USAF legacy fighter. It has a total of 16 chaff and flare dispensers, consisting of 4 ALE-40s in each main landing gear pod and each wing-tip. The dispensers can accommodate either the MJU-11/A magazine (30in x 1in x 1in RR-I70A/AL chaff or M-206 flare cartridges) or the MJU-12/A magazine (15in x 1in x 2in MJU-7 flare cartridges).

Chapter Eight

Flying the Hog

The A-10 is one of the few remaining 'stick and rudder' aircraft still in front-line military service. With only a basic pitch, roll and yaw CAS (control and stability) augmentation system to rely on, smooth flying and the ability to get the aircraft to do what you want it to do are cornerstone abilities that all A-10 pilots must master.

OPPOSITE A pilot exits an A-10C at Kandahar Airfield, Afghanistan, in January 2011. The 75th Expeditionary Fighter Squadron moved their assets to the other side of the flightline, marking the first of many moves towards consolidating the 451st Air Expeditionary Wing's missions. *(USAF)*

ABOVE A pilot from the 358th Fighter Squadron at Davis-Monthan Air Force Base, Arizona, looks over his preflight checklists just before stepping out to the flightline. He was preparing for the second of eight night flights. As part of the A-10C Pilot Initial Qualification course curriculum, he must learn to execute night flying missions using night vision goggles. He'll accomplish this over the next few weeks through six hours of academic classes, five hours in the A-10 flight simulator and eight training flights. *(USAF)*

More complex than flying the A-10 is employing it as a weapons system in combat. At the point at which an A-10 pilot is able to do that, flying the Hog has become a task assigned to muscle memory – something that is truly second nature. In this chapter, Phil Haun – a retired active duty Air Force colonel with over 2,700 hours flying the A-10 – talks us through an actual A-10A combat mission that he flew in 1999. With combat tours in Iraq, Bosnia, Kosovo and Afghanistan, Haun is also author of two authoritative histories of the A-10 (see Bibliography); the views he expresses here are his own and are not those of the US Department of Defense or any of its services.

A-10 Forward Air Controller tactics

'The first flight of the day, Cub 31, is scheduled to arrive on station in the eastern half of Kosovo, codenamed NBA, one hour after dawn. Unlike Misty FACs in Vietnam, who flew two pilots in a single jet, the A-10 FACs fly single-seat in two-ship formations for additional mutual support and firepower.

'The mission commander, Cub 31, is a qualified FAC accompanied by his wingman, Cub 32. A total of four A-10 FAC two-ships are required, two in the east and two in the west, to cover Kosovo for this three-hour vulnerability window. The air tasking order [ATO – the list of missions to be flown that day by all Coalition aircraft] requires three FAC packages during the day, followed by a single night-vulnerability period to be controlled by F-16 FACs.

'In addition to being the FAC-package mission commander, Cub 31 is assigned the duties of embedded Sandy. Should one of the aircraft in the package be shot down, Cub 31 will assume CSAR mission command. These duties are the same as those of the A-1 Sandys in Vietnam: to locate and authenticate the survivor and to suppress any threat to the survivor or the rescue helicopter. Other Sandys

LEFT Signing the forms to take responsibility for the jet, a pilot checks for any write-ups that will indicate potential snags peculiar to this particular aircraft. *(USAF)*

also escort the helicopter in and out of enemy territory. The insertion of Sandys into the FAC package reduces the response time by as much as two hours over the alternative of maintaining A-10 Sandys on strip alert.

'Intelligence has spent the night surfing classified websites in search of potential targets. They have prepared the daily "hog menu du jour", a folder which today is composed of five photographs of Serbian armour and artillery taken by U-2s and national satellites. An additional source of imagery comes from tactical reconnaissance photographs taken by GR-7 Harriers collocated with the A-10s at Gioia del Colle AB in south-eastern Italy. The physical proximity of the two units allows for promising photos to be expedited to the next A-10 before launch. Unfortunately, only one photo of the five is less than 12 hours old, and none has been taken within the last six hours. Six hours is the threshold beyond which most FACs consider it unlikely the target will remain in place. While the Serbs tend to keep their vehicles stationary on clear days, they will relocate them on overcast days and during nights.

'Cub 31 spends several minutes reviewing the frag order, including the special instructions and the banners that accompany the ATO. Changes to the ROE [rules of engagement] are of particular interest. Altitude restrictions have remained fairly constant since the 14 April bombing of a refugee column. That incident has reduced to 5,000ft the minimum altitude FACs may fly to identify targets positively. What has

RIGHT An F-117 Stealth Fighter lifts off from Aviano Air Base, Italy, for a mission over Kosovo in support of NATO's Operation Allied Force. The F-117s were deployed to Aviano as part of the 31st Air Expeditionary Wing. When one F-117 was downed, A-10s provided CSAR cover. *(USAF)*

changed are the restrictions to targets and the process for target approval. No-attack zones within ten miles of the Macedonian border have created a sanctuary that Serbian armour has quickly taken advantage of. Although strikers are still free to attack armour, artillery and AAA, concern regarding NATO cohesion in the face of another collateral damage incident means Cub must now get approval from the CAOC [Combined Air Operations Centre] to attack any trucks.

'After receiving the latest changes, Cub heads for the mass briefing room, an entire wall of which is dominated by a 1:50,000-scale map of Kosovo. On it are marked the latest updates on Serbian activity and NATO strikes from the previous day's missions. After the weather and intelligence briefings, Cub 31 quickly gives the other FACs the plan for the mission.

'Most of the information is already on the line-up cards, courtesy of the squadron's mission planning cell (MPC). Coordination with other aircraft for this mission comes from Aviano AB in northern Italy, where the wing MPC has generated a mission-data card that includes all the aircraft call signs, frequencies, tanker times and tracks and a plethora of deconfliction information required to coordinate many aircraft within such a confined airspace.

'One hour prior to take-off, Cub 31 dons his flight gear and checks out a pair of 12-power space-stabilised binoculars that is his primary means of positively identifying Serbian armour. After meeting his wingman at the duty desk, Cub 31 gets the tail number for his aircraft and a final brief from the squadron supervisor before stepping to the jet.'

A-10 and A-10 FAC-Munitions Load

'The A-10 Warthog is a great choice for an FAC aircraft for several reasons. The greatest advantage lies in its pilots, specifically trained in FAC, CAS and CSAR missions. Most A-10 FACs have more than 1,000 hours in the airframe and have spent that time training to kill armies. The pilot is afforded exceptional visibility and an extensive communications suite of radios that provide UHF (including Have Quick II) and very high frequency amplitude modulation and frequency modulation frequencies. The jet has excellent self-protection capabilities: an ALR-69 radar warning receiver, the ALQ-131 ECM pod, 120 bundles of chaff and 180 flares. In addition, the rugged twin-engine jet is designed to take hits; it comes equipped with a redundant flight-control system and a titanium-armoured cockpit.

'The A-10 – a large fighter aircraft built around a 30mm, tank-killing Gatling gun with a total of 11 hardpoints on its wing – carries a wide variety of munitions. It also carries the Pave Penny pod, a laser spot tracker that indicates in the heads-up display (HUD) the position on which a striker has trained its laser. This enables the FAC to confirm the target before strikers release their bombs. Although the A-10 is assigned primarily to daytime FACing over Kosovo, the jet is the first USAF fighter with an NVG compatible cockpit. Its slow speed, for which it is often maligned, is a tremendous asset in the FAC role, which allows for longer, more accurate looks at targets than can be gained from faster aircraft. Also, the fuel efficiency of its bypass-fan engines gives the jet up to one and one-half hours of loiter time between refuellings. Such features are critical to the success of A-10 FACs in locating Serbian positions.

'The A-10's weapon loadout is custom-built for the FAC mission. On outside stations 1 and 11 hang two AIM-9 heat-seeking missiles and the ALQ-131 ECM pod. The next inboard stations, 2 and 10, carry two rocket pods, each with seven 2.75in Willy Pete rockets. Willy Petes are the primary method of marking targets, as their smoke is easily seen by the naked eye or through a targeting pod. Stations 3 and 9 boast two 500lb, precision-guided AGM-65D Maverick missiles. This IR version of the missile locks on to the heat contrast between the target and its background. The long stand-off range and the 125lb shaped warhead make this fire-and-forget munition ideal against armour.

BELOW The Pave Penny pod juts out into the airflow prominently (right side of the fuselage). Despite the increased sophistication of the A-10C pictured here, the pod remains a valuable tool to the Hog pilot. *(USAF)*

'Centre stations 4, 5, 7, and 8 hold Mk 82 low-drag 500lb general-purpose bombs configured with FMU-113 radar-proximity fuses. Detonation of the bomb at 10–25ft above the ground enhances the fragmentation pattern and is more effective against mobile targets than an impact fuse. Internally, the seven-barrel GAU-8A Gatling gun carries more than 1,100 armour-piercing and high-explosive rounds.

'Although an exceptionally well-constructed CAS aircraft, the A-10 has its weaknesses. It is designed for low-altitude flight, is underpowered at medium altitude, and [in 1999] lacks the technical sophistication of a radar, a GPS navigational system, a data link and a targeting pod. The jet has a high radar cross section that makes it easily detectable by enemy radars, and its slow speed makes it susceptible to AAA and MANPADS [man-portable air defence systems] at low altitude.'

Flight profile of an A-10 FAC

'Upon take-off from Gioia del Colle, Cub begins a turn to the east and climbs to flight level 190 (19,000ft). The flight then contacts Magic, the NATO airborne early warning aircraft responsible for airspace control over the area of responsibility. It takes 45 minutes to cross the Adriatic and reach the tanker track over central Macedonia where a KC-135 is already waiting. After topping off the

RIGHT As can be appreciated from this photo, the A-10 pilot sits high above the canopy sill, giving him excellent visibility to the left and right. Forward visibility is marred by the heavy canopy framing, but the toughened glass and solid construction offer protection from groundfire, which makes the trade-off worthwhile. *(USAF)*

RIGHT Taxiing out to the runway, the pilot's Scorpion helmet-mounted sight is identifiable thanks to the oversized visor. The A-10's nose landing gear supports both taxi and take-off/landing lights, but A-10s have operated in combat at night using neither. *(USAF)*

BELOW In the cold, take-off in the A-10C involves a protracted roll and a little patience. In the hot, and with a combat load, it requires guts! A-10C pilots operating out of Nellis AFB, Nevada, report that coaxing the jet off the runway on the brink of stall is an experience not to be forgotten. *(USAF)*

jets, Cub turns north and contacts Moonbeam [callsign for the Airborne Battlefield Command and Control Center] for the first of their two vulnerability windows.

'Moonbeam relays the CAOC's top two target priorities and confirms that both the required F-16CJ HARM shooters and EA-6B jammers are on station. Cub 31 plots a course to these targets and updates his search plan. The sky over the southern half of the border is clear, but low clouds to the north threaten to blanket the entire valley. Cub 31 arms his weapons, his flares and his electronic self-protection systems as he approaches the border. He begins searching the foothills along the major LOCs as he proceeds to the two CAOC target areas.

'Finding nothing at these locations, he moves on to check out his pre-planned targets and compares the terrain with the target photographs. When these do not pan out, Cub continues to expand his search for the remainder of his 45-minute vulnerability window and looks for any unusual signs that might indicate enemy activity.

'Bear 11, another two-ship of A-10 FACs,

checks in on frequency and takes over control of the eastern half of Kosovo as Cub heads for the second tanker. After refuelling, the flight returns for a second vulnerability window. This sortie is scheduled for a total of 4:0 hours, of which 1:45 will be spent in VR/SC [visual reconnaissance/strike coordination].'

A-10 flight profile, April 1999

Reference time (T Hour)	Take-off time
T minus 2:00	Pre-mission briefing
T	Take-off
T–T+:45	En route to Macedonia tanker track
T+:45–T+1:00	Refuelling (4–5,000lb offload)
T+1:00–T+1:45	Visual reconnaissance/strike control
T+1:45–T+2:15	Refuelling (4–5,000lb offload)
T+2:15–T+3:15	Visual reconnaissance/strike control
T+3:15–T+4:00	Return to base
Total area time	1:45
Total flight time	4:00

BELOW A 52nd Fighter Wing A-10C from Spangdahlem Air Base, Germany, flies off the wing of a 100th Air Refueling Wing KC-135 Stratotanker from RAF Mildenhall, England, during Baltic Region Training Event XII, a multinational NATO exercise in 2012. For the 13 previous years the squadron had been deployed to the Balkans in actual combat operations. *(USAF)*

Threat avoidance

'The primary threat to the A-10 comes from heat-seeking MANPADS. Cub 31 limits this threat by remaining at 15,000ft AGL [above ground level] to the maximum extent possible. When conducting lower-altitude passes (5,000–10,000ft) for target identification, he limits himself to one pass only and uses a combination of jinks and flares when climbing back up to altitude. Cub 32 trails a mile behind, slightly above and offset from Cub 31. As a wingman, Cub 32's purpose is to provide mutual support by covering the lead and calling out all SAM launches. This task is difficult if MANPADS launch because the missiles are extremely fast and their pencil-thin smoke trail is hard to see. Wingmen barely have time to call for flares before the missile zips through the flight.

'As indicated before, one key to avoiding the hundreds of MANPADS spread throughout the Kosovo countryside is to limit the number of passes made on any given target. While this may seem commonsensical, the less obvious reason lies in the limitations of the aircraft. For the underpowered A-10, each pass bleeds off energy in terms of both altitude and airspeed. Diving attacks performed back-to-back leave the jet low, slow and vulnerable to attack during the climb back to altitude.

'For SA-6 operators to get a kill, they must lock-up to the aircraft with the tracking radar and then launch a missile, which homes in on the reflected radar energy bouncing off the aircraft. However, the threat from the SA-6 is greatly diminished by the presence of HARM [high-speed anti-radiation missiles] shooters. An F-16CJ or German ECR Tornado SEAD aircraft can launch HARMs at the SA-6 radar while it is illuminating its target. So the dilemma for the operators becomes whether or not to target strikers and run the risk of being killed.

'For the most part, the SA-6s in Kosovo have remained silent. SA-6 operators have been even more reluctant to fire missiles during the day, when the huge, white smoke plume from the launch and rocket motor creates a prominent trail straight back to the operator's location.

'One A-10 FAC, tongue-in-cheek, believes the biggest threat from an SA-6 launch is the

BELOW An E-8C Joint Surveillance Target Attack Radar System banks to the left following an aerial refuelling. The type has regularly worked with A-10 squadrons to help detect moving targets on the ground, vectoring the Hogs in to identify suspected enemy armour and support vehicles. *(USAF)*

ABOVE The Predator drone came to prominence in 1999, working the airspace over the former Yugoslavia in search of targets to pass to the Hogs that circled below. *(USAF)*

BELOW Several F-16CJ Wild Weasels assigned to the 77th Fighter Squadron 'Gamblers' at Shaw Air Force Base, South Carolina, prepare to take off for an interdiction flight at Aviano Air Base, Italy, in support of Operation Allied Force. The North Atlantic Treaty Organization operation began 24 March 1999, and suspended air strikes against Yugoslavia after its president agreed to withdraw Serb forces from Kosovo. *(USAF)*

potential for a midair collision of fighters in pursuit of the smoke trail, all vying for the kill. This has hardly been the case at night. Although an SA-6 launch is easy to see, its precise whereabouts have proven difficult to locate, even with targeting pods and NVGs.

'AAA is in abundance but easily avoided by staying above 5,000ft. Most of the AAA is 37mm or less, with only a few 57mm pieces and no radar-guided AAA in Kosovo. The only visible signs of AAA fire during the day are the small white clouds that appear as shells explode below the jets.

'Given that, it is still difficult to locate the gun positions. Unlike night-time operations when tracers and muzzle flashes are evident, the use of muzzle flash guards on AAA barrels prevents the daytime sighting of all but the small, brown dust clouds generated as the rounds are fired. Even then, to see the dust kick-up the A-10 FAC must be looking directly at the AAA pit when it is firing. Small arms, on the other hand, have a distinct red muzzle flash, which is easily identifiable, particularly if they are fired from a shaded area. More than one Serbian infantry company has highlighted its position by recklessly firing at A-10s circling overhead.'

Visual reconnaissance and target identification

'The most important quality of a good FAC is the ability to locate targets. A saying among the A-10 FACs is, "95% of tactics is simply finding the target". The same traits that it took to be a good Misty FAC are important to the A-10 FAC. First, it takes hours of visual reconnaissance to get sufficiently familiar with the area to begin to discern Serbian armour and artillery. Although Kosovo is 60 x 60 miles, the Serbian army operates in a relatively small area in and around the larger towns, along the major LOCs, and near the border. Learning where not to look streamlines the VR effort. Pre-mission study of the reported Serbian positions helps to determine where the focus of the day will be. If unsuccessful, the scope can then be increased to widen the search area.

'The key to locating targets is knowing what indicators to look for. The first rule is to note anything unusual or out of place. Clues are as subtle as knowing that Kosovo farmers, when harvesting hay, produce several large bales of hay per field. A field with only one or two large, rectangular hay bales warrants closer inspection and may reveal a tank's main gun barrel protruding through the straw. As the spring rains begin to subside and the ground begins to dry, the night-time movement of the heavy military vehicles produces tracks in the grass. The tan-coloured soil leaves visible tracks in a tank's path. The tracks leading from an empty berm may be used to locate Serb armour hidden in a nearby barn or tree line. In forests, any shape with a 90° angle is suspicious. In addition, the Serbs, knowing A-10 FACs will not strike civilian vehicles, have begun using white buses for transporting troops. A bus parked near a stand of trees is a neon billboard to a smart FAC to begin a search of those woods. Though a trail leading to berms inside a stand of trees may seem well concealed, it actually stands out when viewed from directly overhead. Even Serbian army barracks already destroyed by NATO bombs can be a lucrative location to start a search. The area may still be home to some of the Serbian soldiers, and stray vehicles can be found in and near the compounds. Such insights and trade secrets are often exchanged

ABOVE AND BELOW The Scorpion helmet-mounted monocle sight is clearly visible over the pilot's right eye. While the helmet postdates the combat narrative in this chapter, its use has nonetheless transformed the way that A-10 pilots 'do business' – now spending much more time 'heads up' and looking out of the cockpit. *(USAF)*

ABOVE Just visible on one of the outboard pylons on the port wing of the trailing A-10 is the angular profile of an AAQ-33 Sniper pod. The Sniper offers improved optical and thermal imaging performance allowing the A-10 pilot to detect and identify targets at greater distances. *(USAF)*

BELOW Air Force Joint Terminal Attack Controllers (JTACs) are an elite group of well-trained, very fit and highly capable airmen who are embedded with regular infantry or special forces troops to call in and direct close air support assets, including the A-10. Hog pilots have a special affinity for the JTAC. *(USAF)*

between FACs at the squadron after a mission or at a restaurant during the evening meal.

'Second, a disciplined scan pattern has to be developed along with a proficiency in the use of binoculars. While aircraft vibration makes it difficult to focus high-powered binoculars, the introduction of commercially available, space-stabilised binoculars has alleviated this problem. From 15,000ft it is now possible for a skilled FAC to identify armour and even distinguish between tanks, APCs and self-propelled artillery. With the naked eye, he first selects an area of interest, then concentrates on a specific point for three to four seconds before moving to the next. The binoculars are not used until a potential target has been located. Due to the narrow field of view of binoculars, it takes practice for the FAC to be able to relocate the target while looking through the binoculars. He must first note a nearby prominent landmark to ease the transition before peering through the lens. Likewise, once a target is identified and before the binoculars are put down, the relationship between the target and the landmark is noted. More than one Serbian tank has escaped because of the failure of an FAC to relocate it after lowering his binoculars.

'Third, one flight technique for reducing the

slant range when viewing targets is to keep the jet in a 30° bank, which allows the pilot to search almost directly underneath the jet's flight path. This reduces the slant range by more than a mile in comparison to a level flight path.

'Fourth, some FACs are simply better at finding targets than others. Good mission prep, a positive attitude and keen vision seem to be common denominators of exceptional FACs. Even a highly skilled FAC can use the help of other assets, though, the most important of which are the JSTARS [Joint Surveillance Target Attack Radar System] and the USAF Predator UAV [Unmanned Aerial Vehicle].

'JSTARS is a long-range, air-to-ground surveillance system onboard an E-8C, a modified Boeing 707. It consists of synthetic aperture radar, which is capable of producing a radar image of a selected area, and a moving target indicator (MTI), which is designed to locate slow-moving ground targets. JSTARS has the unique capability of tracking hundreds of vehicles throughout Kosovo with its MTI but lacks a viable onboard target identification system. While JSTARS can view all vehicles moving around Kosovo, it cannot distinguish a T-72 tank from a tractor pulling a trailer loaded with refugees. Collateral damage concerns, which dictate a

visual target identification criterion, greatly reduce the potential utility of JSTARS in this conflict. To overcome this challenge, JSTARS has developed tactics to correlate its tracking data with positive target identification from UAVs and has, on occasion, been able to provide real-time targeting information to FACs.

'While UAVs such as the Predator have been used in the past for surveillance, they also show great promise in locating and identifying targets from low altitude without risk to pilots. Over Kosovo, Predators conducted surveillance and for the first time provided real-time targeting information to the A-10 FACs flying overhead. Effectiveness of the tactics is somewhat limited by the lack of previous Predator experience with FAC procedures, which makes tasks such as altitude deconfliction and target talk-ons difficult. Although UAVs have never been fully integrated into the ATO with strike packages before, operational techniques have quickly been patched together to test their capabilities.

'Qualified ground FACs at the CAOC can now monitor the Predator's video and

conduct target talk-ons directly with A-10 FACs overflying the target area. The occasions when such efforts have proven successful provide a glimpse into the real-time use of UAV platforms with conventional strike aircraft. On one occasion, Moonbeam directed Uzi 11, an A-10 FAC flight, to a specific set of coordinates. Once there, they received a target talk-on from the CAOC's ground FAC to an L-shaped building. Given immediate permission to attack the building, they struck it with three 500lb bombs. Later, when Predator detected Serbian soldiers walking next to the building, the flight was directed to re-attack the site.

'Despite the aid of JSTARS and the Predator, the efforts of Serbian Third Army at concealment and deception continue to complicate target identification.

'The Serbs have placed their armour in such politically sensitive locations as next to churches and inside houses. They have also placed dozens of artillery and armour decoys throughout Kosovo to draw off NATO bombers. Although it is very difficult to tell the difference

between real armour and decoys from altitude, the A-10 FACs have developed a few tactics to compensate.

'The simplest way to determine if a target is a decoy is to blow it up; if there is nothing left of the target afterwards, then it was a decoy. Still other decoys are conspicuous because of their location. If a tank is sitting out in the middle of a field in broad daylight, it is likely a decoy. Another telltale sign is the lack of any fresh track marks or other indications of recent vehicle movement in the area. Again, the only way to know for sure is to blow it up. The thought of wasting munitions, particularly expensive precision-guided weapons, is disconcerting to most FACs. No one wants to make the mission report that they have just killed an inflatable tank decoy with a $100,000 Maverick missile. Still, to pass up on a target simply because it looks too good to be true is self-defeating. There have been many instances of FACs taking a target for a decoy, only to be pleasantly surprised when it sends up a secondary explosion.

'The FAC mission of Swine 01 ended in just

such a discovery on 7 June 1999, two days prior to ceasefire. Locating an incredible ten artillery pieces, Swine directed British Harriers to drop a single Mk 83, 1,000lb bomb on to one of the decoys. When a massive explosion rose up from ammunition stored near the pit, Swine moved in for more kills by attacking and controlling the Harriers and some F-15Es for strikes on all the remaining pits.'

A-10 strike control

'Once Cub 31 has identified a target as valid, he must determine what aircraft and weapons can best be used to attack it. Along with the weapons carried by his flight, there are also NATO fighters scheduled throughout the vulnerability window. These strikers have been given secondary targets on which to drop their bombs if the FAC does not find fresh targets.

'NATO strikers potentially available to Cub come from nine different nations. The arsenal varies greatly from F-15E Strike Eagles carrying LGBs to Italian AMX fighters with neither precision munitions nor a computing weapons delivery system for the Mk 82s they carry. Although B-2 and F-18 aircraft carry the newest GPS munitions, these weapons are not made available to the FAC missions. The majority of strikers are nevertheless fully capable of hitting the targets assigned them. Unlike in Vietnam, where US fighters had difficulty in killing targets that Misty FACs located, once an A-10 FAC identifies a target, it can be destroyed.

'The weapons to be used, then, depend upon the nature of the target found. Precision weapons, such as LGBs or the Maverick, are required against tanks, artillery and AAA. These targets are either armoured or protected by earthen berms and require a direct hit to be taken out. CBU and general-purpose bombs are best used against soft-skinned vehicles and dispersed targets, such as troops in a tree line.

'Cub 31 returns for the second vulnerability window and finds that clouds have moved in and left only the south-eastern part of NBA visible. Cub heads to the city of Gnjilane to

ABOVE Taking gas from a brand new KC-46, this A-10C pilot is no doubt grateful that the tanker crew have not been able to find a cloud to fly into! Refuelling in the A-10 demands an ability to remain focused on a set of visual references on the tanker despite the looming presence of the air-refuelling boom in the pilot's peripheral vision. *(USAF)*

begin a search of the surrounding foothills where there has been previous enemy activity. He locates a row of eight freshly occupied artillery pits and calls up Moonbeam, who quickly lines up a two-ship of CF-18s, call sign Merc 11. The CF-18s are carrying 500lb LGBs.

'Cub passes coordinates, gives them a target area update and begins a talk-on. "Call visual the factory that is just east of the huge town that is on the east–west hardball." G-town (Gnjilane) is the only large town in eastern Kosovo. On the east side of G-town is an enormous factory complex next to the highway that leads east out of the town.

'Merc 11 replies, "Copy. I see one factory. Large structure has a blue roof building to the west." Merc 11 not only responds that he sees the factory but also confirms it by giving a

positive description of a distinct feature. "That's affirmative, let's use that factory east–west one unit. From the eastern edge of factory go two … let's make that three units east on hardball. Then use factory from hardball. You'll see a pull-off on the north side of the hardball. Go one unit to the south off the hardball. In between two small towns you'll see some light revetments." Cub continues the talk-on by setting the length of the factory complex east to west as a unit. He treats that unit as a yardstick and measures the distance along the road to another feature (a pull-off). He talks Merc 11 down between two towns where the artillery is lying.

'Merc 11 responds, "Copy light revetments, there appears to be four to the south and four to five to the north." Merc 11 has the revetments in sight and again gives a

BELOW The F/A-18 first worked alongside during the 1991 Gulf War, when Hog pilots in the scout role found targets and vectored the Hornets in for the kill. In 1999 Canadian CF-18s like this one worked with USAF A-10s in a similar way. *(Royal Canadian Air Force)*

description of what he sees. The revetments appear light due to the light sandy soil in this region of Kosovo in contrast to the darker green grass of the field where the revetments have been dug.

'"Copy. That is affirmative. Say your laser code." Cub wants the laser code to enter in his Pave Penny pod to ensure Merc's laser is actually pointed at the right target. "Laser code is 1,633." Merc is ready to attack and extends to the south-east some ten miles from the target for his run in. Cub clears Merc to drop when he calls inbound.

'Merc shacks (directly hits) the artillery piece. He sets up for a subsequent attack and takes out another piece before running low on fuel and departing.

'In the meantime, Dragon 61 – a two-ship of F-15Es – checks in carrying 500lb LGBs as well. Dragon locks up Cub with his air-to-air radar. Dragon is to call when he has visual on Cub, a fairly easy task, as a two-ship of A-10s circling a target looks like a pair of large Xs in the sky. Dragon calls visual and Cub rolls in to mark, this time with Willy Pete rockets. He shoots three rockets, expecting to get them to blossom into small white phosphorus clouds near the target. As long as Dragon is watching the general target area, he will easily see the smoke generated by the rockets.

'With the A-10's computing weapons delivery system, an accurate rocket can be shot from as

far off as four miles' slant range, which allows Cub to recover well above 10,000ft. He shoots multiple rockets in case one is a dud. He can also refer to the distance between the rockets as an additional unit of measure, if necessary. In this case, though, the rockets land next to the artillery pits. Dragon 61 confirms the smokes, "61 is contact two smokes." "Copy. Look at the further north-east smoke. It's sitting just on the east side of four artillery pits south of a road." Even though the smokes are visible, the artillery pits are so small that Cub has to ensure Dragon has them in sight. Dragon calls contact the target area. Cub is starting to run low on fuel and wants to get the F-15Es dropping as soon as possible. Dragon is not an FAC and therefore not authorised to pick his own target to drop on. He can, however, continue an attack once Cub gives him permission. Cub passes Dragon control of the targets. "You have flight lead control on that target area. I'd like [you] to take out as many of the artillery sites [as you can] at that position. Two have already been struck. Those two are just north of the east–west road." Cub 31 departs for the tanker, and Dragon continues his attack and destroys an additional three artillery pieces. Heading home, Cub 31 contacts Moonbeam and passes on the BDA [battle damage assessment] for his flight and the fighters he has controlled.

'Not all attacks run so smoothly. In this case, these artillery pits were found in an open field

ABOVE Nanoseconds from impact, a GBU-12 500lb laser guided bomb about to leave its mark on a target barge, probably in the Gulf of Mexico near Eglin AFB, Florida. The GBU-12 Paveway III has become a weapon of choice for the A-10 pilot in combat, offering reliability, good weapons effects and great accuracy. *(USAF)*

with little risk of collateral damage. Also, there were no AAA or MANPADS launches seen, although the area is known for having active air defences. Likewise, two sets of precision-bomb-dropping strikers were readily available, native English speakers manned both sets. Though the official language for NATO is English, there is a considerable range of language skills among pilots, with particular difficulties for those from nations such as Turkey and France.'

A-10 strike

'**A**n advantage that Cub 31 has over Misty is the large number of munitions that he and his wingman carry. This gives Cub the

option of destroying targets without having to call in strikers, a capability especially useful against fleeting targets. Although, for the most part, the Serbs do not move their vehicles under clear skies, an occasional mobile APC or tank will be spotted. Other fleeting targets include those in areas where cloud cover is beginning to form. The weather over Kosovo for much of April has been chronically disruptive to strikes. In this case, there may not be time to bring in other fighters before the hole in the clouds closes up. This added flexibility for A-10 FACs has proven a great asset.

'Against armour, the weapon of choice is the AGM-65 Maverick. As long as there is good heat contrast, Cub can fire this 500lb

air-to-surface missile from three to four miles out. The Maverick, while good at killing armour, does not make for a good mark. Too often Cub has to come off target-dry (without firing) because of inadequate contrast. Also, unless the strike produces secondary explosions, the fighters will not be able to see the impact. Cub reserves his Mavericks for armour and other precision deliveries, such as those against dug-in artillery pieces.

'The four Mk 82 airburst bombs that Cub carries are excellent against soft targets. With the computing sight on board, the bombs can be delivered very accurately, even against individual vehicles. They can also be used as marks, adding killing power beyond that of a

rocket. However, the cloud generated from a Mk 82 dissipates rapidly, and unless a fighter is looking directly at the target area at impact he will likely miss the mark. Also, the bomb cloud is darker and provides less contrast than that of a Willy Pete mark.

'The last weapon available to Cub is the 30mm gun, which he uses as his tertiary weapon. As an embedded Sandy, he must reserve half of the rounds for use in case a rescue is required. Also, the extreme slant ranges required at medium altitude greatly reduce the gun's armour-killing potential. To enhance its effectiveness Cub must descend to below 10,000ft. Given the shortage of targets and the wide availability of other weapons, he rarely resorts to the gun.'

Return to base

'Cub lands at Gioia del Colle four hours after departure. Upon landing, the pilots head straight to intelligence. Cub 31 goes to the briefing map and points out all the target areas identified and those attacked. The next set of A-10 FACs are just arriving for their briefing, which allows Cub 31 to take the mission commander aside for an update on the weather in Kosovo and likely target areas. Next, Cubs 31 and 32 must review their HUD videotapes and answer any additional questions for the intelligence mission report. Cub 31 then debriefs his wingman over a sandwich before heading to the hotel for their 12-hour crew rest for tomorrow's mission.'

ABOVE This Hog wears a battered and bruised nose, indicating some scuffed air refuelling 'plugs' by the tanker's boomer. *(USAF)*

RIGHT Marshalling her bird back to parking, this dedicated crew chief will soon be preparing her jet for its next sortie. It's an unspoken rule that the DCC is the owner of the jet and that the pilot is simply allowed to 'borrow it' for the duration of the sortie. *(USAF)*

Chapter Nine

Maintaining the A-10

In 2013, the Air Force calculated that the A-10C cost around $17,500 per hour to operate, a figure that includes fuel, maintenance, and programme upgrades. That figure compares with around $46,000 for the AC-130U gunship and $22,000 for an F-16. One of the main reasons that the A-10 is the cheapest manned tactical asset in the Air Force inventory is because it is so inexpensive to maintain.

OPPOSITE Phase inspection covers around 300 different checks and in peacetime takes many weeks. Here, an A-10 is midway through such an inspection, its panels, slats and other components removed to allow easy access to the aircraft's innards. *(USAF)*

Depot-level maintenance

Designed from the outset to keep depot-level maintenance requirements low, and to allow the Air Force to do all of the normal maintenance inspections and tasks (which is to say that costly contractor support is also minimised), the A-10 has been as much of a success with the maintenance community as it has with the operations community.

The A-10 is so 'field-repair friendly' that the only time it has to go to the depot is for Analytical Condition Inspection (ACI). ACIs are, to quote an Air Force manual, 'in depth condition inspections accomplished on a representative sample of MDS [mission design

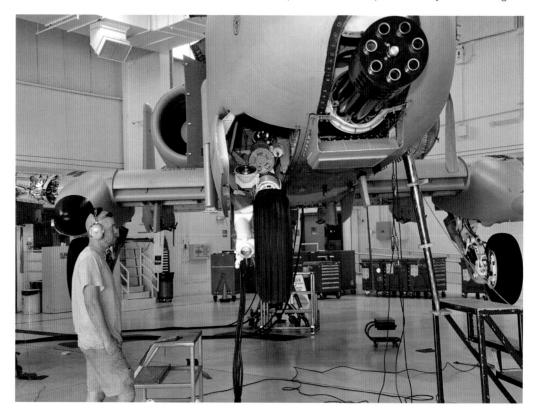

LEFT Increasing avionics complexity has had a corresponding effect on the complexity of A-10 maintenance procedures. Here, an airman uses a tablet to follow a test procedure on the 'glass cockpit' of the A-10C. *(USAF)*

BELOW An A-10C is positioned in an aircraft sling for a lift exercise at Kandahar Airfield, Afghanistan. Crash recovery personnel work with phase crew chiefs to quickly and safely respond to all US aircraft with in-flight emergencies and emergencies on the airfield. *(USAF)*

series] aircraft to uncover hidden defects that are not detected through normal inspection programmes'. In short, the only reason the A-10 has to leave its home base for maintenance is to undergo specialised non-destructive inspections of structural areas, subsystems or parts that are not checked on any periodic basis during normal maintenance.

ACIs were responsible for the discovery of fatigue problems with the A-10's wing, for example. Typically, they result in engineering studies that figure out what fix is necessary and then advise on how to deliver it. Eleven A-10s are selected for ACI annually, and all are sent to Warner-Robins AFB, Georgia, to undergo inspection.

The Air Force's A-10 Systems Engineering Case Study points out that there are, of course, times when the A-10 must make an unscheduled visit to the depot: 'Unscheduled depot repair occurs when an aircraft incident, accident or other unusual occurrence creates a problem beyond the user's ability to correct. Such occurrences result in a request from the MAJCOM [major command] for depot assistance. Depending on the situation, the aircraft may be inducted into a depot or contractor facility, or a depot or contractor field team may be dispatched to the location of the aircraft.'

Of course, the A-10 has become more

ABOVE Maintainers from the 23rd Fighter Group work on the last A-10A+ Thunderbolt II at Pope Air Force Base, North Carolina. This aircraft was later sent to Hill AFB, Utah, for Precision Engagement modification, returning as an A-10C. *(USAF)*

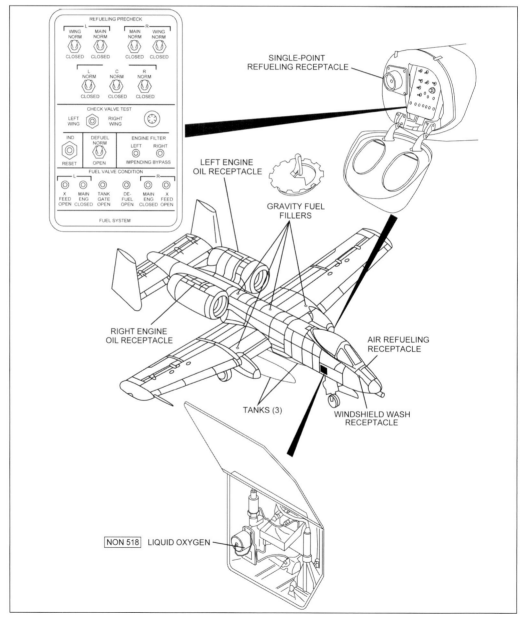

RIGHT AND OPPOSITE The A-10 was successfully designed to be simple to maintain. The servicing diagram for the jet nicely illustrates this, showing the easy access to servicing ports and receptacles including fuel, oil, oxygen, screen wash, air, power and hydraulics. *(USAF)*

difficult to maintain over time thanks to the addition of ever-increasing levels of avionics sophistication. The early 1990s arrival of LASTE, and the 1999 arrival of the EGI and CDU started that ball rolling. While they delivered more capability, they complicated troubleshooting and maintenance requirements. To automate and expedite the maintenance of these complex systems, the Air Force introduced an Operational Test System (OTS) 'to provide a computer test aid for the organisational maintenance units to expedite their maintenance actions. The OTS contains a software test program that requires periodic updates to maintain compatibility with the LASTE and CDU systems,' say Jacques and Strouble. Naturally, the heavily computerised A-10C takes the complexity of A-10 maintenance to a completely new level.

A crew chief's perspective

Having established that the A-10 is not routinely at the depot, what sort of maintenance tasks are performed at unit level? Technical Sergeant Sam Confer is a former F-16C/D maintainer who worked on the 'electric jet' for ten years as a crew chief. His Air

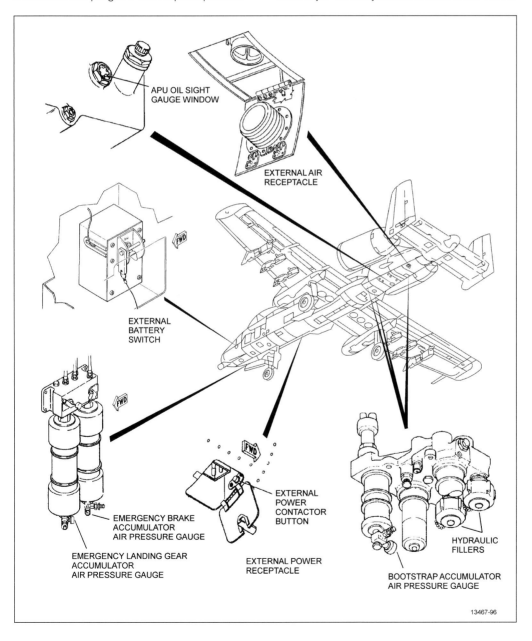

APU OIL SIGHT GAUGE WINDOW

EXTERNAL AIR RECEPTACLE

EXTERNAL BATTERY SWITCH

EMERGENCY BRAKE ACCUMULATOR AIR PRESSURE GAUGE

EMERGENCY LANDING GEAR ACCUMULATOR AIR PRESSURE GAUGE

EXTERNAL POWER CONTACTOR BUTTON

EXTERNAL POWER RECEPTACLE

HYDRAULIC FILLERS

BOOTSTRAP ACCUMULATOR AIR PRESSURE GAUGE

13467-96

National Guard unit moved from the Viper to the Hog, and he has worked on the A-10C for the past six years.

'I'm a Dedicated Crew Chief – a DCC – and my job is to be the aircraft manager. It is the DCC's responsibility to ensure the aircraft is in the best shape possible to complete its daily missions. A DCC works with the production supervisor and other back shops such as Avionics, Weapons or Electro/Enviro, to stay compliant with our scheduled inspections. We also complete unscheduled maintenance in a timely manner to minimise downtime for the aircraft. A DCC is also responsible to train the airmen assigned under them.

'A typical working day for an A-10C DCC starts out with a morning meeting. At this meeting the supervisors will assign crew chiefs to different responsibilities to start the day. Usually, if your jet is flying or has scheduled maintenance you will be assigned to your own jet. If your jet does not have any flying or maintenance scheduled for that day, you will usually be assigned to cover for somebody who is absent or a support function such as end-of-runway [EOR] and LOX [liquid oxygen].

'If your jet is flying, you will grab your forms and review them to make sure nothing is due or written up that would prevent the aircraft from flying. After signing out your tools from the tool room, you head out to the jet.

'Next you are ready to start a preflight inspection. To prepare for the first flight of the day, the crew chief will review the forms to verify there are no discrepancies that would prevent a safe flight. Once at the airplane the crew chief will remove the covers from the aircraft and start his "safe for maintenance". Safe for maintenance is an inspection where you verify that all safety pins are in and all switches in the cockpit are in the off, safe, or norm position. After safe for maintenance is accomplished, the crew chief can then start the actual preflight.

'A preflight inspection is a visual inspection where the crew chief will basically look over the aircraft from front to back, left to right. They are looking for any fluid leaks, broken safety wire, loose fasteners, low fluid levels and low air pressure. Part of the preflight inspection is an engine intake and exhaust inspection. The crew chief will spin the engine blades, looking at each one to make sure that there are no cracked, chipped or distorted blades. After checking tyres for proper air pressure, they will start the APU (auxiliary power unit) and turn on the interior and exterior lights for proper operation. After the preflight, the crew chief signs the forms saying the jet is ready to fly. These forms will be looked over by the expeditor and released for flight at this point.'

With the pilot having arrived at the jet, conducted his own preflight inspection and then signed for the aircraft, the DCC helps him strap into the ACES II seat and stands on fire guard while he starts the APU and the two turbofans. Ready to taxi, the crew chief removes the chocks, marshals him out of his parking space, and smartly salutes.

The pilot then taxis to the EOR. Sam picks up the narrative again: 'EOR stands for end-of-runway inspection. EOR is an area where the jets will stop prior to entering on to the runway. A crew chief will give the jet one last look-over to verify that the crew chief who launched the aircraft did not miss something, such as closing a door or pulling a safety pin. They are also looking for anything that might have broken or started leaking while taxiing to the runway. This is a quick visual inspection that takes about five to seven minutes to complete. After the crew chief says the jet is good, a weapons crew will then go in and pull the safety pins for any

BELOW It's the DCC's responsibility to make sure that the aircraft and its parking place are safe and ready for flight. As these airmen at Bagram Airfield, Afghanistan, demonstrate, that includes clearing snow! *(USAF)*

RIGHT Checking the brake system and attendant hydraulic pressures, this DCC ensures that his Hog is safe to fly. The A-10 has an anti-skid brake system. *(USAF)*

armament that is on the aircraft. The aircraft is now armed and is ready for its mission.'

With the A-10 launched and airborne, Sam's work continues: 'The crew chief will head inside and maybe assist others while waiting for the jet to come back. Most local missions last about 1.5 to 2 hours in duration.

'Upon landing, the aircraft will go to EOR immediately after it leaves the runway, where a weapons crew will meet them and disarm the jet by installing all the weapons' safety pins again. The aircraft will then taxi back to its launch spot, where the crew chief will assist the pilot in taxiing back to his assigned spot. Once stopped, the crew chief will check the brakes and pin the landing gear and leading-edge slats. With the drain bottles installed under the engines, the engines will be shut down.

'In between flights the only servicing that is required is refuelling the aircraft and checking oil. The DCC will perform a "though flight inspection" if the aircraft is going to fly again that day, and if we need to we can add engine oil or add hydraulic fluid. After the through flight the launch and recover process is repeated again.'

LEFT Maintainers 'hot pit' an A-10C belonging to the 81st FS, Spangdahlem AB, Germany. Hot pitting involves refuelling and rearming an aircraft while the pilot remains in the cockpit and the engines continue to run. It's a technique developed specifically for the Cold War, when A-10s killing tanks in the Fulda Gap were expected to be on the ground between sorties for the shortest possible time. *(USAF)*

ABOVE A DCC
marshals out an 81st
Fighter Squadron
A-10C at the EOR.
This 'last chance'
inspection is vital if
hydraulic leaks, fuel
leaks, open panels or
any manner of other
safety of flight issues
are to be detected
before it may be too
late. (USAF)

Inspections

In addition to supporting operational maintenance, Sam provides support for the unit-level inspections. 'There are not actually a lot of hourly inspections. The main hourly inspection is the 500-hour "phase" inspections. Most of the inspections on the A-10 are instead driven by calendar days. Some items driven by calendar-day time-frames are aircraft forms reviews (ADR), aircraft wash, LOX bottle purges and weapon checks.

'Phase inspections are major inspections where the airplane is essentially taken apart and inspected in far more depth than what occurs daily. Many discrepancies that a crew chief finds on daily inspections will be deferred to phase to limit the amount of time a flying aircraft is grounded. The crew chief will work with the phase crew to correct these discrepancies as well as complete the phase inspection cards.'

During the Air Force's high-tempo operations in Afghanistan and Iraq, units would deploy their phase teams in order to continue flying combat missions unabated. For example, the 188th Fighter Wing's phase inspection team, comprising 40 airmen, deployed with the 455th Expeditionary Maintenance Squadron to Bagram, Afghanistan, in summer 2012.

To illustrate that point, A-10Cs are sent to phase inspection after every 500 flying hours. That's a milestone that takes about two years' worth of flying in a stateside ANG A-10 unit, but in Afghanistan in 2012 an A-10 would reach 500 hours nearly every three months.

Master Sergeant Gary Childers, who led that summer 2012 deployment, explained that a phase inspection involves the assessment of 300 separate inspection points and the critical and intrusive nature of phase inspections. Childers revealed that it normally takes teams of eight airmen as long as 30 days to complete a phase inspection on an A-10, but that at Bagram the same team was working 24 hours per day in 12-hour shifts to deliver the same inspection in as little as four days.

Childers explained that 'the A-10 phase team

begins the first day by pulling the aircraft apart, panel by panel, from every direction. Days two and three are spent performing inspections, repairs and reassembly and operational checks to ensure each part functions properly. By day four the aircraft gets a final once-over, and is rolled back out to the flightline for its next mission.'

This rapid accumulation of flight hours translated directly to a rapid accumulation of experience for the maintainers. Childers estimated that his 40-person team were getting a year's worth of training every month. Moreover, the team was also contributing directly to the war effort, and that's something that all DCCs and A-10 maintainers want to do. As Sam Confer put it, 'In my opinion the best thing about working on the A-10 is knowing what its mission is. Knowing your aircraft is built and dedicated to provide close air support gives you extreme pride in what you do, knowing that it could possibly save someone's life. The greatest pride I have as a crew chief is knowing that I have given the pilot the best aircraft possible to complete their mission.'

ABOVE AND BELOW Between sorties, A-10 maintainers check the oil level in each engine. The A-10 is so maintenance friendly that the oil and fuel levels are the only two major measurements that the crew chief must take between sorties. *(USAF)*

Appendix A

A-10C technical specification

General characteristics

Crew: 1.
Length: 53ft 4in (16.26m).
Wingspan: 57ft 6in (17.53m).
Height: 14ft 8in (4.47m).
Wing area: 506ft^2 (47.0m^2).
Airfoil: NACA 6716 root, NACA 6713 tip.
Empty weight: 24,959lb (11,321kg).
Loaded weight: 30,384lb (13,782kg).
CAS mission: 47,094lb (21,361kg).
Anti-armour mission: 42,071lb (19,083kg).
Maximum take-off weight: 50,000lb (23,000kg).
Powerplant: 2 x General Electric TF-34-GE-100A turbofans, 9,065lbf (40.32kN) each.
Internal fuel capacity: 11,000lb (4,990kg).

Performance

Never exceed speed: 450kt (518mph/833kph) at 5,000ft (1,500m) with 18 Mk 82 bombs.
Maximum speed: 381kt (439mph/706kph) at sea level, clean.
Cruise speed: 300kt (340mph/560kph).
Combat radius:
CAS mission – 250nm (288miles/460km) at 1.88 hour loiter at 5,000ft (1,500m), 10 minutes' combat.
Anti-armour mission – 252nm (290miles/467km), 40nm (45miles/75km) sea-level penetration and exit, 30 minutes combat.
Ferry range: 2,240nm (2,580miles/4,150km) with 50kt (55mph/90kph) headwinds, 20 minutes' reserve.
Service ceiling: 45,000ft (13,700m).
Rate of climb: 6,000ft/min (30m/s).
Wing loading: 99lb/ft^2 (482kg/m^2).
Thrust/weight ratio: 0.36.

BELOW An A-10 Thunderbolt II from the 81st Fighter Squadron takes off on a mission against targets in Yugoslavia, 5 April 1999. The A-10 was the first Air Force aircraft specially designed for close air support of ground forces, and its performance stats reflect this fact. *(USAF)*

Appendix B

Persistent CAS and the Hog

The Defense Advanced Research Projects Agency (DARPA) has, since 2011, been working on a persistent close air support (PCAS) programme involving the A-10.

While DARPA had originally envisaged converting the A-10 into an unmanned (or optionally manned) close air support asset, the idea has now been dropped in favour of retaining the pilot in the cockpit. The advantage of the unmanned approach, DARPA had hypothesised, was that by doing away with the mission-planning requirements of humans, an A-10 could be launched and arrive on-station much sooner.

PCAS will digitally link a ground controller with the A-10 pilot, allowing the controller to identify targets and then assign them for engagement. It is broken down into ground and air elements. To engage ground targets, PCAS-Ground (a smart power hub, customised Android tablet loaded with mapping software, a digital radio, and a laser designator) is used by the ground controller to create an engagement plan. The tablet will even allow the controller to interact with the A-10's onboard sensors. The PCAS-Air software installed on another tablet used by the A-10 pilot reads the plan and assigns sensor and weapons resources to it, then shares the information with PCAS-Ground to approve.

While the idea sounds far-fetched, DARPA field-tested some of the ground components of PCAS in Afghanistan during 2012 and 2013, deploying 500 Android tablets equipped with PCAS-Ground situational awareness software, and dramatically

BELOW A freeze-frame from a DARPA promotional video showing the PCAS-Ground software. On the left is the satellite map of the target, on the right the so-called '9-line' tasking that will be transmitted electronically to the A-10 pilot. *(DARPA)*

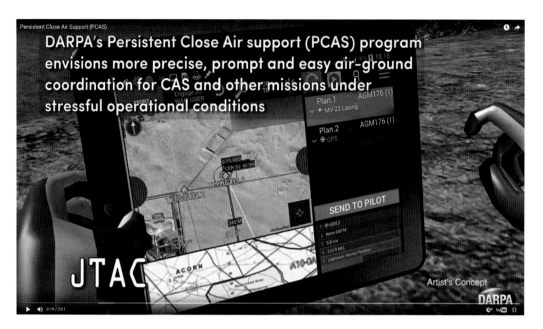

ABOVE Another freeze-frame from the DARPA promotional video. Here, the JTAC has created two attack plans and is about to send them to an MV-22. One plan calls for the MV-22 to lase the target and shoot an AGM-176, the other for it to fire using a set of GPS coordinates. PCAS-Air will automatically assess which of these plans can be executed, based on the resources and assets it knows are available. *(DARPA)*

BELOW The PCAS-Air component consists of a tablet strapped to the A-10 pilot's knee. Here, a Hog driver demonstrates the system in use in a DARPA promotional video. *(DARPA)*

improving the ability of ground commanders to coordinate airstrikes. In fact, in 2015 DARPA demonstrated the entire system in action when US Marine Corps controllers sent an MV-22 Osprey against a target via PCAS-Ground, and the Osprey then engaged the target with an inert AGM-176 Griffin missile.

In June 2015 the first tests of PCAS-Air were undertaken with the A-10. Fifty sorties were flown, culminating in a live fire engagement in which ten targets – generated by ground controllers in as few as three 'clicks' on their PCAS-Ground tablet touch-screens – were struck in six minutes.

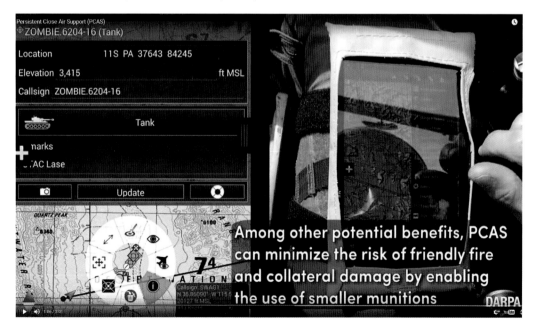

Appendix C

Chopper Popper

On 6 February 1991, Captain Robert Swain downed an Iraqi Bo-105C helicopter, claiming the A-10's first-ever air-to-air kill. He was flying A-10A 77-0205, later christened the 'Chopper Popper', and was assigned to the 706th TFS, 926th TFG.

Swain reported that he'd been engaging Iraqi tanks in central Kuwait, shooting two Mavericks in the process, when he caught sight of movement below him and several miles distant. 'I noticed two black dots running across the desert that looked really different than anything I had seen before. They weren't putting up any dust and they were moving fast and quickly over the desert.'

One of the helicopters headed north and escaped. The other headed south and Swain gave chase. He initially tried to lock up the Iraqi helicopter with an AIM-9, but the Bo-105's heat source was too slight for the missile to track. Instead, he selected the GAU-8: 'I started firing about a mile away. Some of the bullets ran through him, but we weren't sure if it was stopped completely. So I came back with the final pass, hit it and it fell apart. On the final pass, I shot about 300 bullets at him. That's a pretty good burst. On the first pass, maybe 75 rounds. The second pass, I put enough bullets down that it looked like I hit with a bomb.'

BELOW Seven barrels of destruction. The GAU-8/A has a reputation not only for being lethal against tanks, but for being deadly to unwitting aerial adversaries too. *(USAF)*

Appendix D

A-10C weapons list

ABOVE Seen here are the complete ammunition, drive, conveyor, firing and barrel assemblies of the GAU-8/A. When fired, significant vibration is transferred to the airframe ... and in turn to the pilot's eyeballs! *(USAF)*

GAU-8/A Avenger rotary cannon with 1,174 rounds.

BELOW Fairchild Republic A-10A (S/N 73-1668) in flight with two AGM-65 Maverick missiles and four Rockeye cluster bomb dispensers. *(USAF)*

Hardpoints
- 11 with a capacity of 16,000lb (7,260kg).

Rockets
- 4 x LAU-61/LAU-68 rocket pods, carrying 19 x Hydra 70mm or 7 x APKWS rockets.

- 4 x LAU-5003 rocket pods, carrying 19 x CRV7 70mm rockets.
- 6 x LAU-10 rocket pods, carrying each 4 x 127mm Zuni rockets.

Missiles
- 2 x AIM-9 Sidewinder air-to-air missiles.
- 6 x AGM-65 Maverick air-to-surface missiles.

Bombs
- Mk 80 series of unguided iron bombs.
- Mk 77 incendiary munitions.
- BLU-1, BLU-27/B Rockeye II, Mk 20, BL755 and CBU-52/58/71/87/89/97 cluster bombs.
- Paveway LGBs.
- JDAM.
- WCMD.

Other
- SUU-42A/A flares/infrared decoys and chaff dispenser pod.
- AN/ALQ-131 or AN/ALQ-184 ECM pods.
- Lockheed Martin Sniper SE target pod or Litening target pod.
- 600 US gallon (2,300 litre) Sargent Fletcher drop tanks.
- MXU-648 travel pod.
- ASQ-T50 TSTS range pod.
- FACE communication pod.

Appendix E

Survivability

The A-10's survivability is the stuff of legends. Repeatedly throughout its combat operations in Iraq, Afghanistan and the Balkans, it has received damage from enemy fire and made it home.

While much of this good fortune can be attributed to the sheer strength of the A-10 airframe, redundancy in critical systems and a set of manual reversion flight controls have made it possible for the pilot to continue to actually control the aircraft. In this short appendix, the A-10's systems are described in detail.

The hydraulic systems are designed for combat survivability, with the left and right systems physically separated as much as possible. The landing gear, gear uplock, wheel brake and nose-wheel steering lines are isolated from the left system pressure when the gear is up and locked. The landing gear and associated systems can also be isolated from the left hydraulic system. The speed brakes are isolated from right system pressure, and the flaps can be totally isolated from the left hydraulic system.

To actuate the auxiliary landing gear

BELOW A wheels-up landing results in a pranged Avenger barrel assembly and some scratched paintwork, but this Hog won't take long to be returned to flight. The A-10's survivability is legendary. *(USAF)*

ABOVE If an elevator,
elevator actuator
or control path is
jammed, the jammed
side of the system
can be disconnected
by the pilot. Note the
elevator trim tabs on
the outboard side of
the elevator control
surfaces. *(Steve Davies/
FJPhotography.com)*

extension system, the landing gear auxiliary
extension handle is pulled to its stop,
commanding the right hydraulic system
pressure to release the uplocks. If right hydraulic
system pressure is not present, the landing gear
emergency accumulator, located in the nose
wheel well, automatically serves as the pressure
source. This accumulator is pressurised by,
but isolated from, the right hydraulic system.
Upon release of the uplocks, all three gears
will extend by gravity, aided by aerodynamic
forces. Should left hydraulic system pressure be
present, landing gear extension by the auxiliary
system can be accomplished.

The A-10 has shearable flight control
linkages (the elevators are connected by a
shearable crossover shaft, for example). If an
elevator, elevator actuator or control path aft of
the disconnector is jammed, the jammed side
of the system can be disconnected using the
elevator emergency disengage switch. Stick
inputs will then shear the actuator crossover
shaft and the elevator crossover shaft. This will
free the unjammed side of the system. If a jam
occurs with appreciable elevator deflection,
pitch authority in the opposite direction will be
minimal – *eg* if an elevator is jammed with an

upward deflection, pitch down authority will
be reduced.

In instances where there is a dual hydraulic
failure, or when it is expected, a manual
reversion flight control system (MRFCS) gives
the pilot an emergency capability to get the
aircraft back to friendly territory, or at least away
from the threat zone. The mode is adequate
for executing moderate manoeuvres, but the
pilot's manual advises that landing should only
be attempted under ideal conditions or when
ejection is not possible. This is because the
MRFCS mode does not deliver instantaneous
control inputs, and does not provide a full range
of control surface deflection.

Emergency transitions to manual reversion
are automatic and instantaneous in pitch and
yaw, with stick and pedal commands transmitted
directly to the elevator and rudder surfaces
through the actuators, which are in the hydraulic
bypass mode. Transitions in roll must be initiated.
When roll manual reversion is selected, roll control
is transferred from the ailerons to the aileron tabs.
Selecting manual reversion also closes hydraulic
shut-off valves preventing unexpected return to
hydraulic powered flight control. Manual reversion
trim is provided only in pitch.

Appendix F

F: Production numbers

USAF

Some 712 A-10s were built between 1973 and 1982, including six pre-production models. In addition, two YA-10s were constructed in 1971.

BELOW General Electric GAU-8/A installed in the Republic YA-10A. *(USAF)*

1971 Prototypes	YA-10
71-1369	1
71-1370	2
Pre-production serials	**A-10**
73-1664	1
73-1665	2
73-1666	3
73-1667	4
73-1668	5
73-1669	6
Production serials	
75-0258	7
75-0259	8
75-0260	9
75-0261	10
75-0262	11
75-0263	12
75-0264	13
75-0265	14
75-0266	15
75-0267	16
75-0268	17
75-0269	18
75-0270	19
75-0271	20
75-0272	21
75-0273	22
75-0274	23
75-0275	24
75-0276	25
75-0277	26
75-0278	27

75-0279	28	75-0305	54	76-0532	79
75-0280	29	75-0306	55	76-0533	80
75-0281	30	75-0307	56	76-0534	81
75-0282	31	75-0308	57	76-0535	82
75-0283	32	75-0309	58	76-0536	83
75-0284	33			76-0537	84
75-0285	34	76-0512	59	76-0538	85
75-0286	35	76-0513	60	76-0539	86
75-0287	36	76-0514	61	76-0540	87
75-0288	37	76-0515	62	76-0541	88
75-0289	38	76-0516	63	76-0542	89
75-0290	39	76-0517	64	76-0543	90
75-0291	40	76-0518	65	76-0544	91
75-0292	41	76-0519	66	76-0545	92
75-0293	42	76-0520	67	76-0546	93
75-0294	43	76-0521	68	76-0547	94
75-0295	44	76-0522	69	76-0548	95
75-0296	45	76-0523	70	76-0549	96
75-0297	46	76-0524	71	76-0550	97
75-0298	47	76-0525	72	76-0551	98
75-0299	48	76-0526	73	76-0552	99
75-0300	49	76-0527	74	76-0553	100
75-0301	50	76-0528	75	76-0554	101
75-0302	51	76-0529	76		
75-0303	52	76-0530	77	77-0177	102
75-0304	53	76-0531	78	77-0178	103

YA-10A (71-1370) in flight. *(USAF)*

A-10A (73-1667) during an in-flight refuelling test. *(USAF)*

77-0179	104	77-0201	126	77-0223	148
77-0180	105	77-0202	127	77-0224	149
77-0181	106	77-0203	128	77-0225	150
77-0182	107	77-0204	129	77-0226	151
77-0183	108	77-0205	130	77-0227	152
77-0184	109	77-0206	131	77-0228	153
77-0185	110	77-0207	132	77-0229	154
77-0186	111	77-0208	133	77-0230	155
77-0187	112	77-0209	134	77-0231	156
77-0188	113	77-0210	135	77-0232	157
77-0189	114	77-0211	136	77-0233	158
77-0190	115	77-0212	137	77-0234	159
77-0191	116	77-0213	138	77-0235	160
77-0192	117	77-0214	139	77-0236	161
77-0193	118	77-0215	140	77-0237	162
77-0194	119	77-0216	141	77-0238	163
77-0195	120	77-0217	142	77-0239	164
77-0196	121	77-0218	143	77-0240	165
77-0197	122	77-0219	144	77-0241	166
77-0198	123	77-0220	145	77-0242	167
77-0199	124	77-0221	146	77-0243	168
77-0200	125	77-0222	147	77-0244	169

77-0245	170		78-0593	213		78-0637	257
77-0246	171		78-0594	214		78-0638	258
77-0247	172		78-0595	215		78-0639	259
77-0248	173		78-0596	216		78-0640	260
77-0249	174		78-0597	217		78-0641	261
77-0250	175		78-0598	218		78-0642	262
77-0251	176		78-0599	219		78-0643	263
77-0252	177		78-0600	220		78-0644	264
77-0253	178		78-0601	221		78-0645	265
77-0254	179		78-0602	222		78-0646	266
77-0255	180		78-0603	223		78-0647	267
77-0256	181		78-0604	224		78-0648	268
77-0257	182		78-0605	225		78-0649	269
77-0258	183		78-0606	226		78-0650	270
77-0259	184		78-0607	227		78-0651	271
77-0260	185		78-0608	228		78-0652	272
77-0261	186		78-0609	229		78-0653	273
77-0262	187		78-0610	230		78-0654	274
77-0263	188		78-0611	231		78-0655	275
77-0264	189		78-0612	232		78-0656	276
77-0265	190		78-0613	233		78-0657	277
77-0266	191		78-0614	234		78-0658	278
77-0267	192		78-0615	235		78-0659	279
77-0268	193		78-0616	236		78-0660	280
77-0269	194		78-0617	237		78-0661	281
77-0270	195		78-0618	238		78-0662	282
77-0271	196		78-0619	239		78-0663	283
77-0272	197		78-0620	240		78-0664	284
77-0273	198		78-0621	241		78-0665	285
77-0274	199		78-0622	242		78-0666	286
77-0275	200		78-0623	243		78-0667	287
77-0276	201		78-0624	244		78-0668	288
			78-0625	245		78-0669	289
78-0582	202		78-0626	246		78-0670	290
78-0583	203		78-0627	247		78-0671	291
78-0584	204		78-0628	248		78-0672	292
78-0585	205		78-0629	249		78-0673	293
78-0586	206		78-0630	250		78-0674	294
78-0587	207		78-0631	251		78-0675	295
78-0588	208		78-0632	252		78-0676	296
78-0589	209		78-0633	253		78-0677	297
78-0590	210		78-0634	254		78-0678	298
78-0591	211		78-0635	255		78-0679	299
78-0592	212		78-0636	256		78-0680	300

78-0681	301	78-0698	318	78-0715	335
78-0682	302	78-0699	319	78-0716	336
78-0683	303	78-0700	320	78-0717	337
78-0684	304	78-0701	321	78-0718	338
78-0685	305	78-0702	322	78-0719	339
78-0686	306	78-0703	323	78-0720	340
78-0687	307	78-0704	324	78-0721	341
78-0688	308	78-0705	325	78-0722	342
78-0689	309	78-0706	326	78-0723	343
78-0690	310	78-0707	327	78-0724	344
78-0691	311	78-0708	328	78-0725	345
78-0692	312	78-0709	329		
78-0693	313	78-0710	330	79-0082	346
78-0694	314	78-0711	331	79-0083	347
78-0695	315	78-0712	332	79-0084	348
78-0696	316	78-0713	333	79-0085	349
78-0697	317	78-0714	334	79-0086	350

A-10A (80-222) of the 18th Tactical Fighter Squadron, 343 Composite Wing, at the wash rack. *(USAF)*

79-0087	351	79-0104	368	79-0121	385
79-0088	352	79-0105	369	79-0122	386
79-0089	353	79-0106	370	79-0123	387
79-0090	354	79-0107	371	79-0124	388
79-0091	355	79-0108	372	79-0125	389
79-0092	356	79-0109	373	79-0126	390
79-0093	357	79-0110	374	79-0127	391
79-0094	358	79-0111	375	79-0128	392
79-0095	359	79-0112	376	79-0129	393
79-0096	360	79-0113	377	79-0130	394
79-0097	361	79-0114	378	79-0131	395
79-0098	362	79-0115	379	79-0132	396
79-0099	363	79-0116	380	79-0133	397
79-0100	364	79-0117	381	79-0134	398
79-0101	365	79-0118	382	79-0135	399
79-0102	366	79-0119	383	79-0136	400
79-0103	367	79-0120	384	79-0137	401

An A-10 Thunderbolt II lands after a mission.
A-10s provided close-air support in Operation
Enduring Freedom in Afghanistan. *(USAF)*

79-0138	402	79-0182	446		
79-0139	403	79-0183	447	80-0140	490
79-0140	404	79-0184	448	80-0141	491
79-0141	405	79-0185	449	80-0142	492
79-0142	406	79-0186	450	80-0143	493
79-0143	407	79-0187	451	80-0144	494
79-0144	408	79-0188	452	80-0145	495
79-0145	409	79-0189	453	80-0146	496
79-0146	410	79-0190	454	80-0147	497
79-0147	411	79-0191	455	80-0148	498
79-0148	412	79-0192	456	80-0149	499
79-0149	413	79-0193	457	80-0150	500
79-0150	414	79-0194	458	80-0151	501
79-0151	415	79-0195	459	80-0152	502
79-0152	416	79-0196	460	80-0153	503
79-0153	417	79-0197	461	80-0154	504
79-0154	418	79-0198	462	80-0155	505
79-0155	419	79-0199	463	80-0156	506
79-0156	420	79-0200	464	80-0157	507
79-0157	421	79-0201	465	80-0158	508
79-0158	422	79-0202	466	80-0159	509
79-0159	423	79-0203	467	80-0160	510
79-0160	424	79-0204	468	80-0161	511
79-0161	425	79-0205	469	80-0162	512
79-0162	426	79-0206	470	80-0163	513
79-0163	427	79-0207	471	80-0164	514
79-0164	428	79-0208	472	80-0165	515
79-0165	429	79-0209	473	80-0166	516
79-0166	430	79-0210	474	80-0167	517
79-0167	431	79-0211	475	80-0168	518
79-0168	432	79-0212	476	80-0169	519
79-0169	433	79-0213	477	80-0170	520
79-0170	434	79-0214	478	80-0171	521
79-0171	435	79-0215	479	80-0172	522
79-0172	436	79-0216	480	80-0173	523
79-0173	437	79-0217	481	80-0174	524
79-0174	438	79-0218	482	80-0175	525
79-0175	439	79-0219	483	80-0176	526
79-0176	440	79-0220	484	80-0177	527
79-0177	441	79-0221	485	80-0178	528
79-0178	442	79-0222	486	80-0179	529
79-0179	443	79-0223	487	80-0180	530
79-0180	444	79-0224	488	80-0181	531
79-0181	445	79-0225	489	80-0182	532

80-0183	533	80-0227	577	80-0271	621
80-0184	534	80-0228	578	80-0272	622
80-0185	535	80-0229	579	80-0273	623
80-0186	536	80-0230	580	80-0274	624
80-0187	537	80-0231	581	80-0275	625
80-0188	538	80-0232	582	80-0276	626
80-0189	539	80-0233	583	80-0277	627
80-0190	540	80-0234	584	80-0278	628
80-0191	541	80-0235	585	80-0279	629
80-0192	542	80-0236	586	80-0280	630
80-0193	543	80-0237	587	80-0281	631
80-0194	544	80-0238	588	80-0282	632
80-0195	545	80-0239	589	80-0283	633
80-0196	546	80-0240	590		
80-0197	547	80-0241	591	81-0939	634
80-0198	548	80-0242	592	81-0940	635
80-0199	549	80-0243	593	81-0941	636
80-0200	550	80-0244	594	81-0942	637
80-0201	551	80-0245	595	81-0943	638
80-0202	552	80-0246	596	81-0944	639
80-0203	553	80-0247	597	81-0945	640
80-0204	554	80-0248	598	81-0946	641
80-0205	555	80-0249	599	81-0947	642
80-0206	556	80-0250	600	81-0948	643
80-0207	557	80-0251	601	81-0949	644
80-0208	558	80-0252	602	81-0950	645
80-0209	559	80-0253	603	81-0951	646
80-0210	560	80-0254	604	81-0952	647
80-0211	561	80-0255	605	81-0953	648
80-0212	562	80-0256	606	81-0954	649
80-0213	563	80-0257	607	81-0955	650
80-0214	564	80-0258	608	81-0956	651
80-0215	565	80-0259	609	81-0957	652
80-0216	566	80-0260	610	81-0958	653
80-0217	567	80-0261	611	81-0959	654
80-0218	568	80-0262	612	81-0960	655
80-0219	569	80-0263	613	81-0961	656
80-0220	570	80-0264	614	81-0962	657
80-0221	571	80-0265	615	81-0963	658
80-0222	572	80-0266	616	81-0964	659
80-0223	573	80-0267	617	81-0965	660
80-0224	574	80-0268	618	81-0966	661
80-0225	575	80-0269	619	81-0967	662
80-0226	576	80-0270	620	81-0968	663

A newly modified A-10C taxis in during the roll-out ceremony at Davis-Monthan Air Force Base, Arizona, on 29 November 2006. *(USAF)*

81-0969	664	81-0986	681	82-0650	697
81-0970	665	81-0987	682	82-0651	698
81-0971	666	81-0988	683	82-0652	699
81-0972	667	81-0989	684	82-0653	700
81-0973	668	81-0990	685	82-0654	701
81-0974	669	81-0991	686	82-0655	702
81-0975	670	81-0992	687	82-0656	703
81-0976	671	81-0993	688	82-0657	704
81-0977	672	81-0994	689	82-0658	705
81-0978	673	81-0995	690	82-0659	706
81-0979	674	81-0996	691	82-0660	707
81-0980	675	81-0997	692	82-0661	708
81-0981	676	81-0998	693	82-0662	709
81-0982	677			82-0663	710
81-0983	678	82-0647	694	82-0664	711
81-0984	679	82-0648	695	82-0665	712
81-0985	680	82-0649	696		

Acronyms and abbreviations

A – Attack.

AAA – Anti-aircraft artillery.

AB – Air Base.

AC – Alternating current.

ACI – Analytical Condition Inspection.

AE – Armed Escort.

AEF – Air Expeditionary Forces.

AEG – Air Expeditionary Group.

AFAC – Airborne forward air controller.

AFAL – Air Force Armament Laboratory.

AFB – Air Force Base.

AFRC – Air Force Reserve Command.

AFRes – Air Force Reserve.

AGL – Above ground level.

AIR – Air Inflatable Retard bomb.

ANA – Afghan National Army.

ANG – Air National Guard.

AoA – Angle of attack. The angle of the wing as it cuts through relative airflow.

APC – Armoured personnel carrier.

API – Armour-piercing incendiary round.

APKWS – Advanced Precision Kill Weapon System.

APU – Auxiliary power unit.

AR – Armed Reconnaissance.

ASD – Aeronautical Systems Division.

ATAF – Allied Tactical Air Force.

ATO – Air tasking order.

ATS – Air turbine start.

BAI – Battlefield air interdiction.

BRAC – Base Realignment and Closure.

C2 – Command and control.

CAF – Combat air force.

CAOC – Combined Air Operations Centre.

CAS – Close air support; also Control And Stability System.

CDU – Control display unit.

CEP – Circular error probable.

CETADS – Comprehensive Engine and Trending Acquisition Database.

CFP – Concept Formulation Package.

CG – Centre of gravity.

CMWS – Common Missile Warning System.

CPP – Competitive Prototype Phase.

CSAR – Combat search and rescue capability.

CSF – Close Support Fire.

DARPA – Defense Advanced Research Projects Agency.

DC – Direct current.

DCC – Dedicated Crew Chief.

DSMS – Digital Stores Management System.

DU – Depleted uranium.

EAC – Enhanced Attitude Control.

ECM – Electronic countermeasures.

ECS – Environmental control system.

EFS – Expeditionary Fighter Squadron.

EGI – Embedded GPS-INS.

EO – Electro-optical.

EOR – End-of-runway.

EPU – Electronic processor unit.

ESPS – Emergency Stall Prevention System.

EW – Electronic warfare.

F – Fighter.

FAC – Forward Air Control; also Forward Air Controller.

FLIR – Forward-looking infrared.

FOL – Forward Operating Location.

FOV – Field of view.

FS – Fighter Squadron.

ft – Feet.

ft/min – Feet per minute.

FW – Fighter Wing.

FY – Fiscal year.

g – Measure of gravitational force.

GCAS – Ground Collision Avoidance System.

GE or GEC – General Electric Company.

GPS – Global positioning system.

HARM – High-speed anti-radiation missiles.

HARS – Heading Attitude Reference System.

HD – High Drag bomb.

HE – High explosive.

HEI – High explosive incendiary.

HOTAS – Hands-on throttle and stick.

hr – Hours.

HUD – Heads-up display.

Hz – Hertz.

IADS – Integrated Air Defence System.

IAM – Inertially aided munition.

IDG – Integrated drive generator.

IEPU – Improved Electronic Processor Unit.

IFFCC – Integrated Flight and Fire Control Computer.

IIR – Imaging infrared.

in – Inches.
INS – Inertial Navigation System.
IOC – Initial Operational Capability.
IR – Infrared.
IS – Islamic State.
ISAF – International Security Assistance Force.
ITT – Interstage turbine temperature.
JAWS – Joint Attack Weapons System.
JDAM – Joint direct attack munitions.
JSTARS – Joint Surveillance Target Attack Radar System.
JTAC – Joint Terminal Air Controller.
kg/m² – Kilograms per square metre.
KIAS – Knots indicated airspeed.
kN – Kilonewtons force.
kph – Kilometres per hour.
KSTAR – Surveillance and Target Attack Radar System.
kt – Knots.
LANTIRN – Low-altitude navigation, terrain following infra-red for night.
LASTE – Low-Altitude Safety and Targeting Enhancement.
lb – Pounds.
lbf – Pounds-force.
lb/ft² – Pounds per square foot.
LDGP – Low-Drag General Purpose bomb.
LGB – Laser Guided Bomb.
LJDAM – Laser Joint Direct Attack Munition.
LOC – Location.
LOX – Liquid oxygen.
m – Metres.
MANPADS – Man-portable air defence systems.
MLG – Main landing gear.
mm – Millimetres.
MMH/FH – Maintenance man-hours per flying hour.
MPC – Mission Planning Cell.
mph – Miles per hour.
MRFCS – Manual Reversion Flight Control System.
m/s – Metres per second.
MTI – Moving target indicator.
n/a – Not applicable.
NATO – North Atlantic Treaty Organization.
N/AW – Night/Adverse Weather.
NBC – Nuclear, biological, chemical.
NLG – Nose landing gear.
nm – Nautical miles.
NVG – Night vision goggles.
NWS – Nose-wheel steering.
OBOGS – On-board oxygen generating system.

ODS – Operation Desert Storm.
OEF – Operation Enduring Freedom.
OFP – Operational Flight Program.
OIR – Operation Inherent Resolve.
OOD – Operation Odyssey Dawn.
OSW – Operation Southern Watch.
OTS – Operational Test System.
PAC – Pitch attitude control.
PAVE – An invented acronym subsequently used for 'precision avionics vectoring equipment'.
PCAS – Persistent close air support.
PE – Precision Engagement programme.
PFCS – Primary Flight Control System.
psi – Pounds per square inch.
RAD – Requirements Action Directive.
RFP – Request for proposal.
ROVER – Remote Operational Video Enhanced Receiver.
rpm – Revolutions per minute.
RWR – Radar warning receiver; pronounced 'raw'.
SADL – Situational awareness data link.
SAM – Surface-to-air missile.
SAS – Stability Augmentation System.
SCL – Standard combat loadout.
SGGI – Secondary gun gas ignition.
SOF – Special Operations Forces.
SPO – System Program Office.
TAC – Tactical Air Command.
TASS – Tactical Air Support Squadron.
TEMS – Turbine Engine Monitoring System.
TES – Test and Evaluation Squadron.
TFS – Tactical Fighter Squadron.
TFTS – Tactical Fighter Training Squadron.
TFW – Tactical Fighter Wing.
TGP – Target pod.
TTW – Tactical Training Wing.
UARRSI – Universal Aerial Refueling Receptacle Slipway Installation.
UAV – Unmanned Aerial Vehicle.
UHF – Ultra-high frequency.
USAF – United States Air Force.
USAFE – United States Air Force Europe.
VFR – Visual flight rules.
VR – Visual reconnaissance.
WCMD – Wind-corrected munitions dispenser.
WOW – Weight on wheels.
WP – White phosphorous.
WS – Weapons School.
WSO – Weapons System Officer.

Bibliography

A-10s over Kosovo: The Victory of Airpower over a Fielded Army as Told by the Airmen Who Fought in Operation Allied Force, Colonel C.E. Haave and Lieutenant-Colonel P.M. Haun (Air University Press, 2003).

A-10 Thunderbolt II (Warthog) Systems Engineering Case Study, David R. Jacques PhD, Lieutenant-Colonel USAF (Retired) and Dennis D. Strouble PhD (Air Force Center for Systems Engineering, 2010).

A-10 Thunderbolt II Units of Operation Enduring Freedom 2008–15, Gary Wetzel (Osprey Publishing, 2015).

Airpower versus a Fielded Force: Misty FACs of Vietnam and A-10 FACs of Kosovo – A Comparative Analysis, Lieutenant-Colonel P.M. Haun (Air University Press, 2004).

'Warthog News, The Ultimate Modern A-10 Thunderbolt II Reference', http://warthognews.blogspot.co.uk/ and https://www.facebook.com/warthognews/.

An A-10C from Eglin Air Force Base, Florida, flies along the coast of Florida on 25 March 2010 during the first flight of an aircraft powered solely by a biomass-derived jet fuel blend. *(USAF)*

Index